# VOICE OVER

sound and vision in current art

# VOICE

sound and vision in current art

# OVER

National Touring Exhibitions

sbc

Published on the occasion of *Voice Over: Sound and Vision in Current Art*, a National Touring Exhibition organised by the Hayward Gallery, London for the Arts Council of England

Exhibition tour:

Arnolfini, Bristol
31 January – 22 March 1998
Hatton Gallery, Newcastle
4 April – 17 May 1998
Nottingham Castle Museum and Art Gallery
12 September – 1 November 1998

Exhibition curated by Michael Archer and Greg Hilty
Exhibition organised by Greg Hilty and Marisa Culatto
Education material devised by Helen Luckett

Catalogue designed by Society
Printed by Leycol Printers Ltd

Cover: Joseph Grigely, *Untitled Conversation (Paula's Birthday Party)*, 1996 (detail), ink on paper tablecloth



ISBN 1 85332 170 2



National Touring Exhibitions, Hayward Gallery and Arts Council Collection publications are distributed by Cornerhouse Publications, 70 Oxford Street, Manchester M1 5NH (tel. 0161 237 9662; fax. 0161 237 9664).

# FOREWORD

In recent years National Touring Exhibitions has organised a number of thematic exhibitions, grouping contemporary artists together in ways intended to highlight important and unexplored features of current artistic practice. *Outer Space*, curated by Yve Lomax and shown in 1991-92, looked at some of the fictions surrounding photographic work and included slide and video installations. *Wall to Wall*, curated in 1994 by Maureen Paley, invited different artists to make site-specific works at three galleries in three cities. The present exhibition, *Voice Over: Sound and Vision in Current Art*, consists of work made through the 1990s which tries, using radically different means, to articulate the 'voice' as a primary transmitter of artistic meaning.

Within the recent fashions for multi-media and multi-culturalism, there has been a remarkable surge of activity linking cultural identity with the status of the artwork itself. This relationship comes across through an obvious play between the author of the work and its subject, and across a range of media – film, video, sound and installation, as well as more traditional forms – assembled to complement or to stand in for each other. *Voice Over* concentrates on the interplay between sound and vision. It considers the 'voice', understood not so much as the meaning of a work of art, but as the way that meaning is determined by the means through which it is conveyed. This focus raises questions of articulation, of what is declared and what is left unspoken, and of mining for meaning in both the personal and collective subconscious. It brings an element of time into the visual in a particularly potent way, and also allows rich narrative structures to develop, using techniques that include, among others, sampling and polyphony.

*Voice Over* has been curated by Michael Archer, writer and lecturer, and Greg Hilty, Senior Curator at the Hayward Gallery. The two worked together previously on *Material Culture: the Object in British Art of the 1980s and '90s*, which was presented at the Hayward Gallery in the spring of 1997: although concentrating on sculptural work, that exhibition also strongly featured sound, which was used by artists as a material and as a means of activating space. *Voice Over* emerged out of that collaboration but has taken a distinct direction of its own. Michael Archer, in his lucid essay, outlines this direction by looking at the work shown in a wider cultural context.

This catalogue also contains the direct voices of its participating artists, who have all responded to specific questions put to them by the curators to help elucidate the role of 'the voice' in their work. We are, as ever, enormously grateful to all nine artists, those who have agreed to present existing work in a new and experimental context – Jeremy Deller, Stan Douglas, Lucy Gunning, Bethan Huws and Juan Muñoz – and those who have made new work with the exhibition in mind – Tacita Dean, William Furlong, Joseph Grigely and Ross Sinclair.

I would also like to thank all those who have helped facilitate the participation of these artists, including Rose Lord of Frith Street Gallery, Robin Klassnik and Simon Morrissey of Matt's Gallery, Jeannie Freilich of Marian Goodman Gallery, New York, Martin McGeown of the Cabinet Gallery and Amy Vogel. Colin Griffiths, assistant to Stan Douglas, has played an invaluable role in realising the work *Hors-champs*. We are also grateful to Tom Cullen for installing the audio-visual work in this exhibition, and to MITES for their continuing co-operation in maintaining the Hayward Gallery's audio-visual equipment.

We are grateful to all lenders to the exhibition, including Carol and Arthur Goldberg.

Last, but far from least, I would like to express my sincere thanks to the venues participating in the tour of *Voice Over*, whose enthusiasm for and collaboration on this exhibition have been most welcome through all stages of its development and organisation. In particular I thank Tessa Jackson and Denise Robinson of Arnolfini, Bristol, Martyn Ladds and Andrew Burton of the Hatton Gallery, Newcastle, and Kate Stoddart of Nottingham Castle Museum and Art Gallery.

Susan Ferleger Brades
Director, Hayward Gallery

# INTRODUCTION

*Michael Archer*

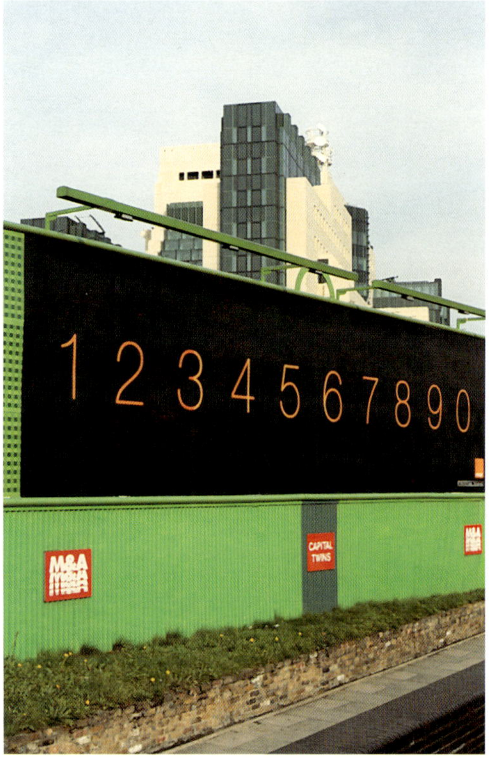


Orange
*Numbers* national poster campaign,
October – November 1994
Courtesy Orange™

Works of art which incorporate the use of sound can be difficult to exhibit. They do not keep to their own portion of space with the requisite seemliness, but spill out into the surrounding area. They make their presence felt throughout a gallery. You can still hear them while you are looking at, or listening to, something else. The traditional solution to this problem has been to subdivide the space with screens, building separate boxes to keep each sound in. But what if the problem is not thought of as a problem at all? What if it is taken as a positive factor, something to work with in the conception of an exhibition?

*Voice Over* is an attempt to do this. It brings together work by nine artists which embodies, presents or alludes to a sense of the voice. It is not, therefore, just a sound show, although there is some sound in it. It is installed in as open a way as each venue allows, making a virtue of the ability of some works to permeate the gallery spaces. It is polyphonic and features the voice in several modes, among them conversational, declamatory, intimate, expressive, collective and individual. Sometimes, for social, physical or aesthetic reasons, the voice is either silent or absent. It is no less discernible for that. The question of how the other senses contribute to and support a primarily visual experience is one which *Voice Over* raises without wishing to provide a single, definitive answer.

A recent advertisement, part of an early campaign for Orange mobile phones, shows the ten digits from 1 through to 0 printed in orange in a plain sans-serif typeface on a black background. In looking at this ad we could, of course, read the numbers in turn from one end of the line to the other, but their familiarity and simplicity of form make it possible for us to apprehend the whole row at once, as an image. A strictly numerical progression would start at zero. Here, by contrast, the shift of 0 from the beginning to the end of the sequence suggests something quite different: a telephone keypad. The black rectangle becomes a sublime space containing the possibility of all the telephone calls and fax transmissions that have ever been or will ever be sent, as well as all the others that might only be imagined. The image suggests universality but nevertheless emphasises the specificity and intimacy of each and every one of those calls.

It takes only a moment's reflection to realise that the information we receive through our different senses is not kept apart in the mind. We can grasp the qualities of a surface, for example, because we understand how it would feel under our fingers. Likewise, seeing a billboard displaying the Orange poster lets us hear the voices of many. Maurice Merleau-Ponty explains this phenomenon in saying:

> *The senses intercommunicate by*
> *opening onto the structure of a thing.*
> *One sees the hardness and brittleness*
> *of glass, and when, with a tinkling*
> *sound, it breaks, this sound is conveyed*
> *by the visible glass.*[1]

Although quite distinct from the clinical condition of synaesthesia, in which sensory information of one kind is confusingly experienced across all modes, the same term is applied within the visual arts. The interest in synaesthesia of the late nineteenth-century Symbolists rested on the belief that an experience expressed in terms of one sense could well be grasped through another. Wassily Kandinsky's later investigations into the relationship between sound and colour are another well-documented instance.[2] Even without being as explicit as Kandinsky, however, it is clear from their shared technical and descriptive vocabulary – composition, harmony, tone, chromaticism, vibrancy, resonance – that expression and communication in the auditory and visual fields are closely linked.

Sensory interconnectedness may be an unvarying feature of the way in which the body functions, but the manner in which that capability makes itself visible in art is constantly changing. The availability of technologies of reproduction, such as film, video and sound recording, has been one stimulus to such change. In particular, the appropriation of these technologies by artists has altered our appreciation of the way in which time functions in the work of art. The narrative within, say, a painting, is seen all at once. Insofar as it unfolds in response to prolonged viewing, it does so within the endless present of the discrete, separate space of the picture. A work incorporating video, film or audiotape, on the other hand, requires a certain given time to reveal itself. The time of the work and the real time of the spectator in viewing it flow into and out from one another.

This effect has implications for all art, not just for that which directly employs electronic media. Some of the works in *Voice Over* make a noise, others do not. Presence and absence come up against one another in a variety of ways. Whatever the case – a disembodied voice, a palpable silence, a physical representation of speech, a disjunctive combination of image and sound – an understanding of the work is gained through a process of sensory interplay that develops over time. 'Synaesthesia', writes video artist Bill Viola, 'is the natural inclination of the structure of contemporary media.'[3]

For *The Singing Lesson*, 1994 (cat. 6), Lucy Gunning bought herself a singing lesson and, over the space of an hour, was taught the rudiments of a technique of which she was largely ignorant. We can witness the interchange that took place during that lesson on two video monitors, one showing the teacher, the other Gunning. Both screens chart the same period of time, but they are out of sync. What the teacher hopes for is not immediately delivered. For all her desire to increase the emotional, intellectual and physical control she has over the process of enunciation, Gunning is unable to produce the voice her teacher wishes to hear at the moment she wishes to hear it.

It is curious that in order to say what we want to say with our own voices, it helps to receive instruction. The individuality of the voice is not denied but rather enhanced by such training. Jean-Francois Lyotard uses the word 'timbre' to refer to the specificity of the voice. The recognition of a particular, distinct quality introduces us to a presence. This experience of presence, Lyotard says, is more than the simple perception of being here, now; it is to be confronted by matter, by something other than oneself.[4] The double aspect of attraction and repulsion felt in the face of the materiality of another's existence is seen in Tacita Dean's *Magnetic*, 1997 (cat. 1). In this seven-part work Dean has used film sound stock to record a range of sounds produced by the body – a kiss, a wolf whistle, an 'um'. That she has done this we must, to an extent, take on faith because the sounds are not heard. Instead, Dean gives us the strips of magnetic tape on which each of them has been recorded. Affection, appreciation and thoughtful hesitation are physically present as symbols of the body that signalled them. None of the sounds could be described as speech, yet they all contribute to the larger picture of the body as a vehicle for communicative expression. Grouped together and mounted in frames, the sixty-eight sounds constitute a poetic representation of the human form that reverberates in several sensory dimensions at once. Our ability to distinguish between, for example, a spit and an expectoration, grows out of an awareness of several differences: namely, those between the lengths of tape used to record the two actions, the length of the respective words written in chinagraph pencil on those pieces of tape, and the contexts provided by the other sounds with which each is grouped.

In a previous work, *Foley Artist*, 1996, Dean conducted a celebratory deconstruction of the subtle art of building up a soundtrack to lay alongside a visual film sequence. Film requires the viewer to construct for him- or herself a complete world from the two separately crafted elements of image sequence and soundtrack. The appearance or effect of authenticity is purchased only at the price of much artifice. The appearance of authenticity, though, is not its actuality. There is a gap between the two that cannot be wished away. Juan Muñoz struggles with the existence of this gap, making figures that aspire, but never quite manage, to attain the status of people capable of giving voice to their own identity. Muñoz's ventriloquist's dummies, mannequins and other figures occupy or create stage-like settings, and for all that their titles imply speech – *The Prompter*, 1988 or the *Conversation Pieces* of the late 1980s and early 1990s, for instance – they remain silent. Sometimes, as with *Neal's Last Words*, 1997, the mannequin's mouth moves, although the only sound to be heard is the faint hum of a motor. Very much in this spirit, the silence of *Ventriloquist Looking at a Double Interior*, 1988 (cat. 8) is disturbing, almost conspiratorial. A small figure (a ventriloquist's dummy rather than a ventriloquist) sits atop a broad plinth-cum-wall facing two drawings. The corner of a chair seen in both indicates that they could be different views of the same space. Doorways open into other rooms as the eye travels into the depths of each picture. Jointly they depict a grand and complex interior, but one that is ominously empty. Even the armchair in the foreground – the one in which the ventriloquist might be expected to sit in order to balance the dummy on his knee – remains vacant.

In many cases in *Voice Over*, works come into being through the offering of a space to others in which to speak. Audio Arts, Jeremy Deller, Joseph Grigely, Bethan Huws and Stan Douglas all do this in their various ways. The voices in their works are multiple, though the character of each within the collective is quite distinctive.

William Furlong's long-time strategy with Audio Arts has been to make recordings of conversations with people in the place where he is to exhibit. People who are stopped in the street and asked simple questions about their daily habits, likes and dislikes reveal much about the character of their dwelling place. Accent, speech patterns, vernacular phrasings and references to local issues and nearby landmarks thus constitute Furlong's material. Working on this material back in his studio, Furlong uses sampling, repetition, juxtaposition and layering to build a polyvocal representation of the identity of the location itself. Played back in the exhibiting gallery, the final, richly-textured sound work, such as *Spoken For/ Spoken About*, 1998 (cat. 4) in *Voice Over*, allows the place to speak and to be listened to by those who move through it. The voice is specific to the site and, when the exhibition travels to the next venue, new recordings are made in the new location.

Jeremy Deller adopts something of the role of curator in encouraging fans of the pop group, Manic Street Preachers, to offer their homages to the band for assembly into the installation, *The Uses of Literacy*, 1997 (cat. 2). The title refers to the 1957 book in which Richard Hoggart considers what is good and valuable in our language and literature, what is useful and productive to know and learn, and what, through ignorance, avoidance or laziness, might lead to the debasement of culture. Forming an attachment to pop music is still widely regarded as something people do instead of exploring the real or proper riches of their culture. What the Manic Street Preachers' fans demonstrate in their work (and in their conversation about it recorded by Audio Arts which subsequently became part of the installation) is that, far from standing in opposition, the two strands of cultural appreciation are integrally connected. In spite of his 'advantage' in terms of age and experience, Deller's unwillingness to assert himself over the fans leaves room for them to reveal how, through the inspiration to read and think offered by the group's music and lyrics, they are searching for and beginning to find their own voice.

Joseph Grigely's deafness makes explicit the reality that the art work is a site for and of communication. The writings of others, made in the process of dialogue with him, introduced into tableaux and spatial arrangements, sometimes alongside texts of his own, engender a strong sense of the work as a focus for the generation of and meditation upon meaning (cat. 5). Grigely's wall works and installations are not merely representations of the act of conversing. They are conversations as objectified reality, social intercourse conducted by means of exchange other than the common one of speech. In writing of Grigely's work, artist Aaron Williamson has described deafness as a 'physical adjustment'. It only appears to be a disability because of 'the consensus within the language of speech'.[5] In conversation, Grigely speaks in similar terms. He is used to situations in which he speaks and his hearing interlocutor has to write everything down. The strangeness of the activity for the hearing person forces the reappraisal of the assumptions that underlie communication. In one such conversation with me, Grigely retold one of the Deaf community's mythological joke scenarios, in which a deaf person and a hearing person, conversing through writing, are joined by a third, hearing person. Later, the deaf person leaves, turning at the door to see the two who remain continuing to converse in silence, writing notes back and forth.

In extending an invitation to the Bulgarian vocal group, the Bistritsa Babi, to perform on a Northumberland beach, Bethan Huws sets up a complex scene of shifts and displacements. The singers come from a mountainous area of eastern Europe. Their songs have grown out of that place but, in singing them on a shoreline off the western coast of the continent, they articulate Huws's own sense of distance from her native Wales. Insofar as it is not Huws casting songs on the outgoing tide, she is in a literal sense absent from the work. Yet in her absence we recognise the understated generosity with which she welcomes the voices of the Bistritsa Babi into her work. A further layer of complexity is added in Huws's short film, *Singing for the Sea*, 1993 (cat. 7). This is not a substitute for the original performance, entitled *The Bistritsa Babi – A Work for the North Sea*, July 1993, since every showing of the film is a genuine sounding of its own. However, it is much more than an echo from another source.

There is one soundtrack to Stan Douglas's *Hors-champs*, 1992 (cat. 3), but a double-sided screen presents two possible visual narratives as accompaniment to it. The 'authorised' version of a jazz session, edited from recordings made on two cameras, is backed by its negative: all the out-takes run together in a sequence that necessarily spans exactly the same period of time. Both show a group of American musicians who left the US in the 1960s and settled in Europe. In part, they moved to escape the draft, but there was another, equally important reason: the kind of music they were playing did not receive widespread attention or favour at home, and the journey to Europe was made in search of a more sympathetic audience. For Douglas, the use of jazz music in *Hors-champs* is doubly important. Firstly, the fundamentally improvisatory nature of free jazz is seen as symptomatic of the social forces behind the civil rights movement in the US during the 1960s. In this context the music's rejection of an imposed form speaks against repression. Secondly, it is a statement of opposition to western musical orthodoxy. In his book, *Philosophy of Modern Music*, Theodor Adorno criticises jazz for the way in which it makes a fetish of rhythm and indulges in the extreme mechanics of music-making – what he refers to as 'a fiddling and tooting'.[6] A critique of this kind, which pits formal and technical innovations considered significant against the decadence of jazz, effectively denies that black musicians in the west had any voice at all in modern music. They were, literally and metaphorically, placed *hors champs*, out of play. It is impossible to see both screens in *Hors-champs* at once. A choice must be made. In making that choice the viewer is forced to consider how what is being seen affects the meaning of what is being heard.

A voice sounds in the space that it makes as it sounds. The musicians in *Hors-champs*, for example, like the Bistritsa Babi singing to the North Sea, or the young pop fans of *The Uses of Literacy*, are not merely finding a place from which to make utterance. They are bringing that place into being through their actions. Part of the process of establishing this place lies in the identification of a community, a group of people who, as a consequence of shared values and attitudes, speak as you do. The folk songs of Scotland that Ross Sinclair sings in his stage-like constructions are the material substrate of a national sense of identity in the absence of which his ability to utter at all would be seriously called into question. *Dead Church/Real Life*, 1998 (cat. 9) plays upon the interdependence of personal and communal qualities in the voice. A small, bright red, church-shaped structure lies on its side in the corner of the gallery. Inside this structure a monitor plays a video of Sinclair singing hymns. The tape runs backwards, thereby marking a distance from the specifically religious message of the words – something with which Sinclair feels little empathy – while not losing the overall sense of the melodic power of the tunes. As usual, Sinclair sings with his back to the camera, stripped to the waist in order to show the tattooed words, 'Real Life', across his back.

A church designed in vernacular style represents, in its form, the voice of the people. In *Dead Church/Real Life*, Sinclair shows the ambivalence of his relationship to this population and the words it speaks. As with Muñoz, the authenticity of what we see and hear is difficult to determine. In life as in art, in order to communicate what we wish to say, we have to borrow words from a shared language. This places us in constant debt to the world in which we speak, but it is also the very thing that makes it possible for others to comprehend our thoughts and feelings.

Notes

1 Maurice Merleau-Ponty, *The Phenomenology of Perception*, Routledge, London, 1962, p. 229

2 See, for example, Kandinsky's stage composition *The Yellow Sound* in K. Lankheit (ed.), *The Blaue Reiter Almanac*, Thames and Hudson Ltd, London, 1974, p. 207ff

3 Bill Viola, 'The Sound of One Line Scanning' in D. Lander and M. Lexier (eds), *Sound by Artists*, Art Metropole, Ontario, 1990, p. 49

4 Jean-Francois Lyotard, *The Inhuman*, Polity, 1991, p. 140

5 Aaron Williamson, review of *Joseph Grigely* at the Anthony d'Offay Gallery, Art Monthly, May 1996, p. 36

6 Theodor Adorno, *Philosophy of Modern Music*, Sheed & Ward, London, 1973, p. 199

# THE ARTISTS

# TACITA DEAN

1
*Magnetic*, 1997
Magnetic tape and chinagraph
Dimensions variable
Courtesy the artist and Frith Street Gallery, London

Tacita Dean was born in 1965 and studied at Falmouth College of Art from 1985 to 1988. In 1989 she won the Greek Government Scholarship to the Supreme School of Fine Arts in Athens, and on her return to London in 1990 enrolled at The Slade School of Fine Arts. Dean's first solo exhibition, *The Martyrdom of St Agatha and Other Stories*, took place in Slovenia in 1994, and since then she has had solo exhibitions in Bourges (France), New York, Rotterdam and London (in the Art Now room at the Tate Gallery in 1996, and most recently at Frith Street Gallery). Dean's work has been included in numerous group exhibitions including the *British Art Show 4*. A solo touring exhibition of her work will start at the ICA Philadelphia in autumn 1998. She lives and works in London.

## What is the relation between sound and image in your work?

In film, the sound and the image are recorded and processed separately; they are only brought back together in the editing process. In video, the sound and the image are recorded together, and the action is in separating them. My interest resides in this gap between the sound and the image: the mistakes that are made when the two fall out of sync, or the uninvited event of a sound unintentionally colliding with an image. I require sound to have its own autonomy. We hear sound differently when it is apart from the image. In cinema, the sound is as laboured a fiction as the picture, but we all too often disregard it as accompaniment. Its effect on what we see, however, is radical and is totally instrumental in dictating the meaning of the image on the screen.

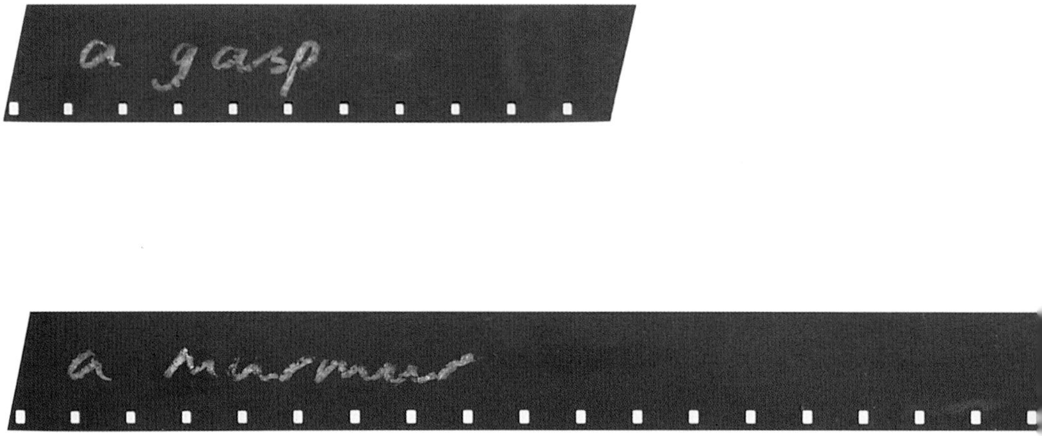


*Magnetic*, 1997 (detail)
Detail from *A Breath (Magnetic)*
Magnetic tape and chinagraph
Courtesy the artist and Frith Street Gallery, London
Photo: Steve White

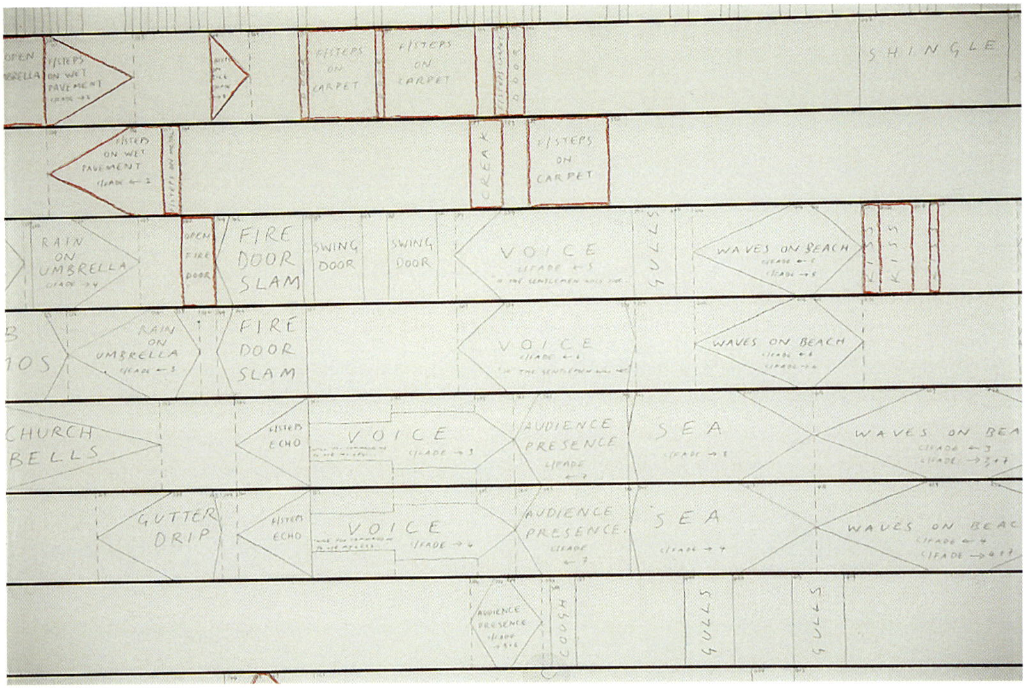


*Foley Artist*, 1996
Dubbing cue sheet (opposite and detail above)
71 x 410 x 22 cm
Installation in the *Art Now* room, Tate Gallery, 1996
Courtesy the Artist and Frith Street Gallery, London
Photo: Tate Gallery

DUBBING CUE SHEET

# JEREMY DELLER

2
*The Uses of Literacy*, 1997
Mixed media
Dimensions variable
Private collection
Courtesy Cabinet Gallery

Jeremy Deller was born in 1966. In 1988 he completed a BA in Art History at the Courtauld Institute, London, specialising in Baroque Art and Architecture. In 1992 he completed an MA degree in Art History at Sussex University. *Home Alone* in 1993 (Dulwich, London) was his first solo show; others include *Migrateurs* at the Musée d'Art Moderne de la Ville de Paris in 1996, and *The Uses of Literacy* at the Norwich Art Gallery in 1997. Deller has taken part in many group shows including *Life/Live* in Paris and Lisbon and *Poppoccultural* at the South London Gallery. He has initiated many projects including a T-shirt for Agnès B, personal ads in *The Guardian* and *The Daily Telegraph*, and a number of Acid Brass performances in the UK and abroad. He lives and works in London.

Whose voices are present in *The Uses of Literacy*?

Claudia Schmölders
Sara Jayne
Abi Rivitt
Katherine Fitzgerald
Diana Jarvis
Loryma Cunningham
Sarah Meadham
Edward Meadham
Darren Francis
Donna Marshall
Stephanie Cross
Adèle
Lotte Peterson
Melanie Rawlinson
Jennifer Turnbill
Ali Williams
Katy Dermody
Sylvie Leithgoe
Claire Rice
Lisa Massey
Joanne Scholes
Emma Bourne
Lucy Bryson
Scott Glover
Aishling
Krisha Barnsby
Angela Davis
Siobhan
Bernadette Sheridan
Rachel
Marie Masters
Goranka
Beeza
Andrew Wilkinson
Stephen Neal
Sarah Prybylska
Alison C.
Vicky Turner
Kat
Vicki Garmant

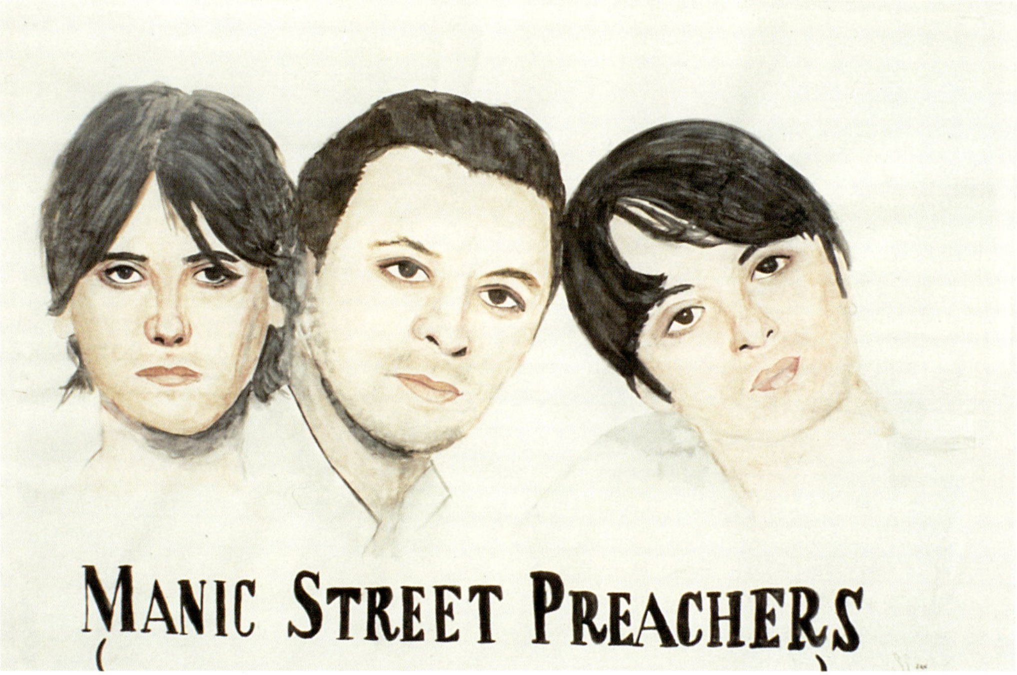


(above)
*The Uses of Literacy*, 1997 (detail)
Sarah Jayne, *Manic Street Preachers*
Private collection, courtesy Cabinet Gallery
Photo: Jeremy Deller

(opposite)
*The Uses of Literacy*, 1997
Installation view at CCA Glasgow
Private collection, courtesy Cabinet Gallery
Photo: Will Bradley

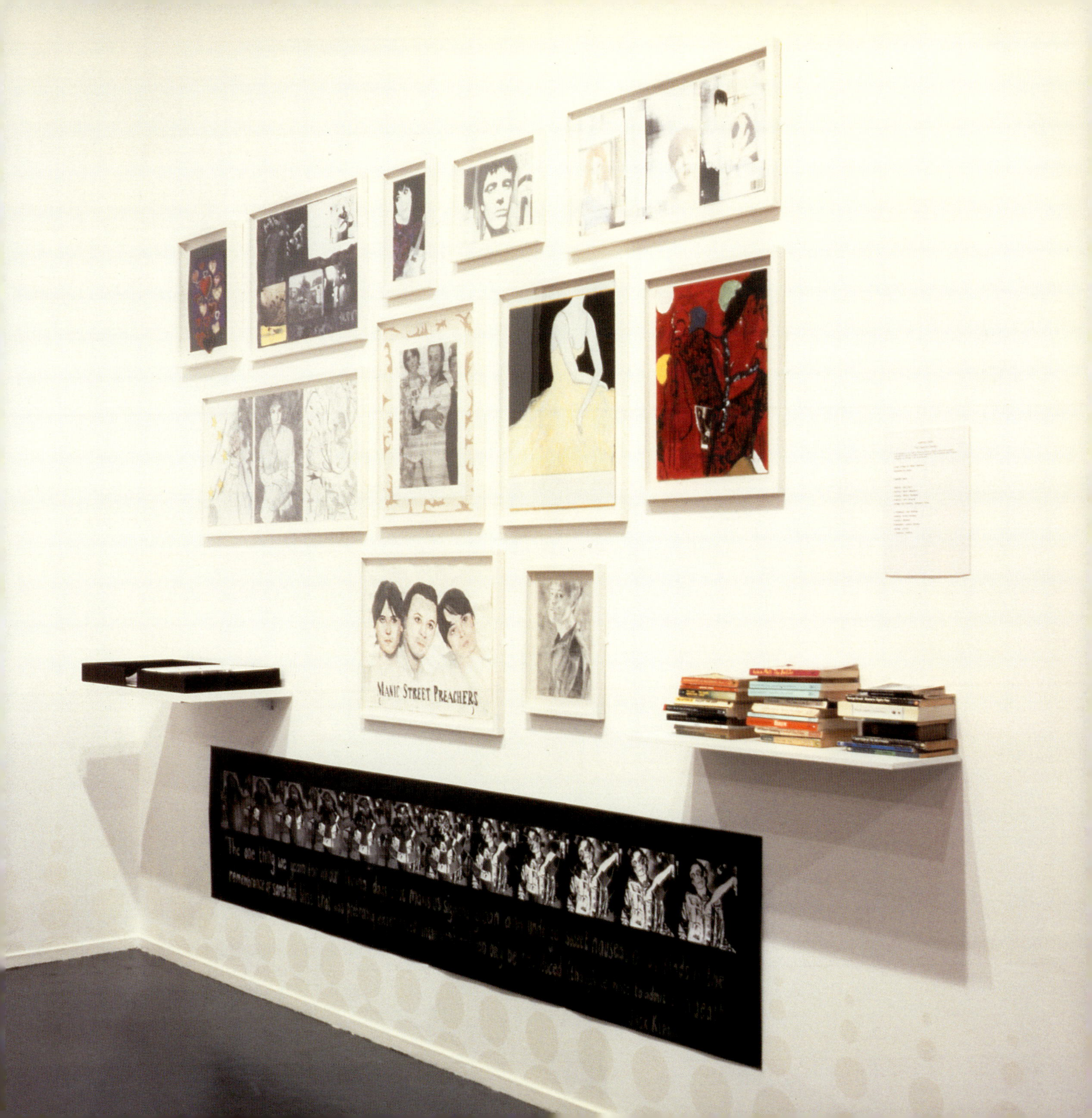
MANIC STREET PREACHERS

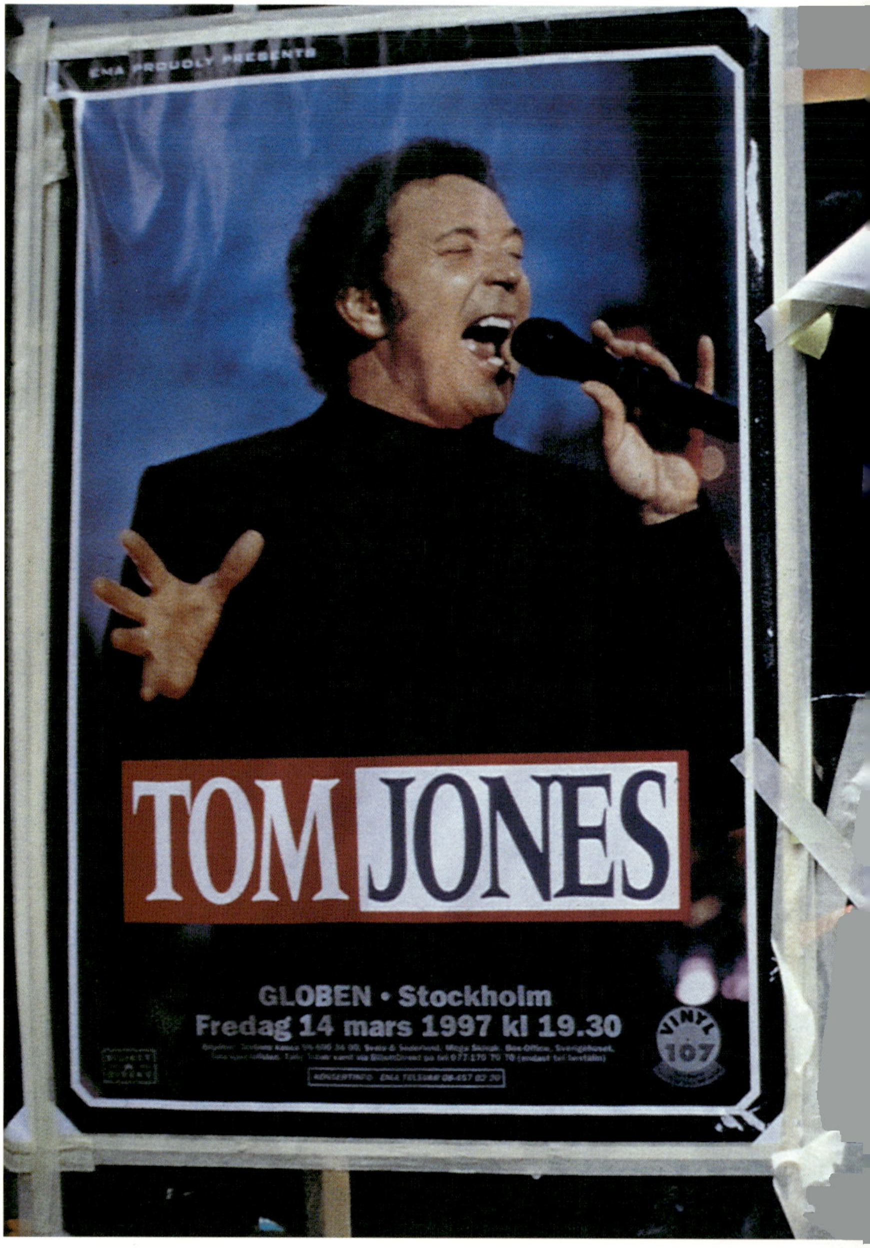


*Poster*, 1997 (Stockholm)
The artist
Photo: Jeremy Deller

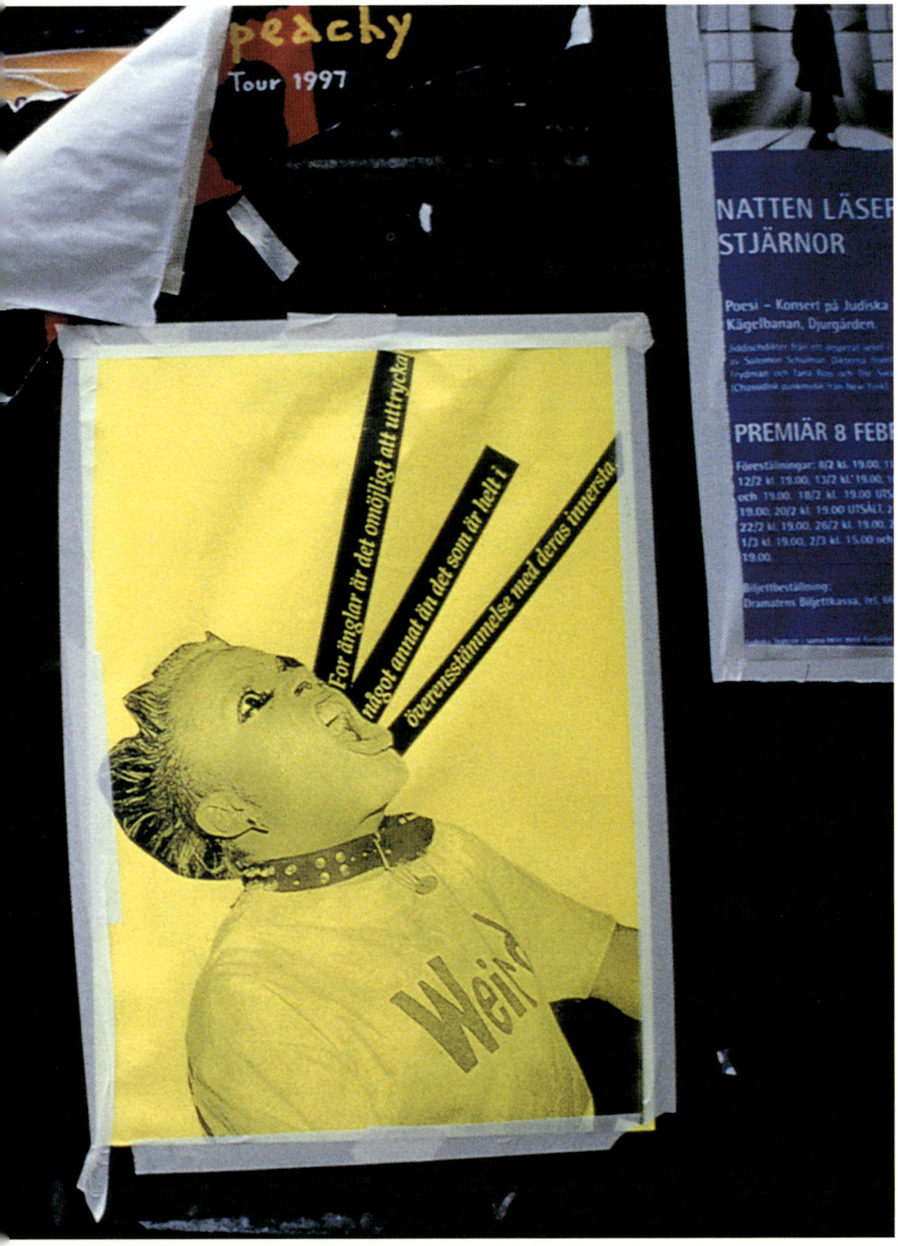
peachy
Tour 1997
NATTEN LÄSER
STJÄRNOR
Poesi – Konsert på Judiska
Kägelbanan, Djurgården
PREMIÄR 8 FEB
För änglar är det omöjligt att uttrycka
något annat än det som är helt i
överensstämmelse med deras innersta

# STAN DOUGLAS

3
*Hors-champs*, 1992
Installation
Laserdisc projections on double-sided screen
Dimensions variable
The artist

Stan Douglas was born in 1960 in Vancouver where he still lives. He attended the Emily Carr College of Art, Vancouver 1982. He has exhibited widely in Canada, the USA, Europe, Japan, Korea, Australia, South Africa and, most recently, Venezuela. In 1994 the Centre Georges Pompidou mounted a major survey of his work which then travelled to Madrid, Zurich and Rotterdam. He has participated in many group exhibitions including *Hall of Mirrors: Art and Film since 1945*, Museum of Contemporary Art, Los Angeles in 1996, and in *Documenta X, Sculpture. Projects in Münster*, the Lyon Biennale and the Johannesburg Biennale in 1997. In 1988 Douglas curated an exhibition and edited a publication of *Samuel Beckett: Teleplays*. Among his projects for 1998 is a two-person show with Douglas Gordon at the Dia Center for the Visual Arts, New York.

## How does music speak in *Hors-champs*?

What was typically known as 'the New Thing' in the United States and as 'Free Jazz' in Europe was an idiom of Afro-American music characterized by simultaneous group improvisation and relative harmonic freedom. Because of the metaphor clearly embodied in its formal premise and (to be exact) the political commitments of many 'Free' players, the music was generally associated with black nationalism in the US - but in France, during the late 1960s and early 1970s, the music acquired other connotations. It was, for example, so popular with the Mai 1968 generation that audiences for Free Jazz concerts could number in the thousands, and there were even festivals organized by the French Communist Party, which regarded the music as an ideal of social organisation. By the end of the 1970s, the music's popularity had begun to wane, perhaps because of these extrinsic associations. Although musical ideas from the period remain important today, the legacy of Free Jazz is partially obscured by the revisionism and revivalism that had been so overwhelmingly prominent throughout the 1980s.

*Hors-champs* presents the performance of four American musicians who either lived in France during the Free Jazz moment, or who still reside there today: George Lewis (trombone), Douglas Ewart (saxophone), Kent Carter (bass) and Oliver Johnson (drums). Their presence in that country may be considered continuous with the history of black American musicians emigrating to France, which extends back at least as far as the arrival of Josephine Baker and Sydney Bechet on European soil. The music they play is based on Albert Ayler's 1965 composition, *Spirits Rejoice*, and is composed of four basic musical materials: a gospel melody, an attenuated call and response, a heraldic fanfare and *La Marseillaise*. The latter's similarity to the fanfare underlines its origin in military music, and, like many other national anthems such as *Star Spangled Banner* (which also makes a brief appearance), the recollection of its blood-thirsty lyric will remind one of the the tacit content of myths of national identity.

*Hors-champs* was shot *en direct* in the style of an ORTF [French national television] musical television production from the same era as Ayler's composition - notably those of Jean-Christophe Averty. This accounts for the rough *chiaroscuro* and abstract placelessness of its *mise-en-scène*. However, while those French television productions typically used four or five cameras, we used only two: one operated by Serge Godet and the other by myself. Two video projections are simultaneously presented on recto and verso sides of a suspended wall. While one side of the screen shows a 'program' montage of the two cameras, the other presents a simultaneous counter-narrative of everything that had been edited out.

This project was produced at the Centre Georges Pompidou by Musée national d'art moderne, Paris. Rehearsals began during the week of 29 April 1992. *Hors-champs* is dedicated to the people of South Central Los Angeles.

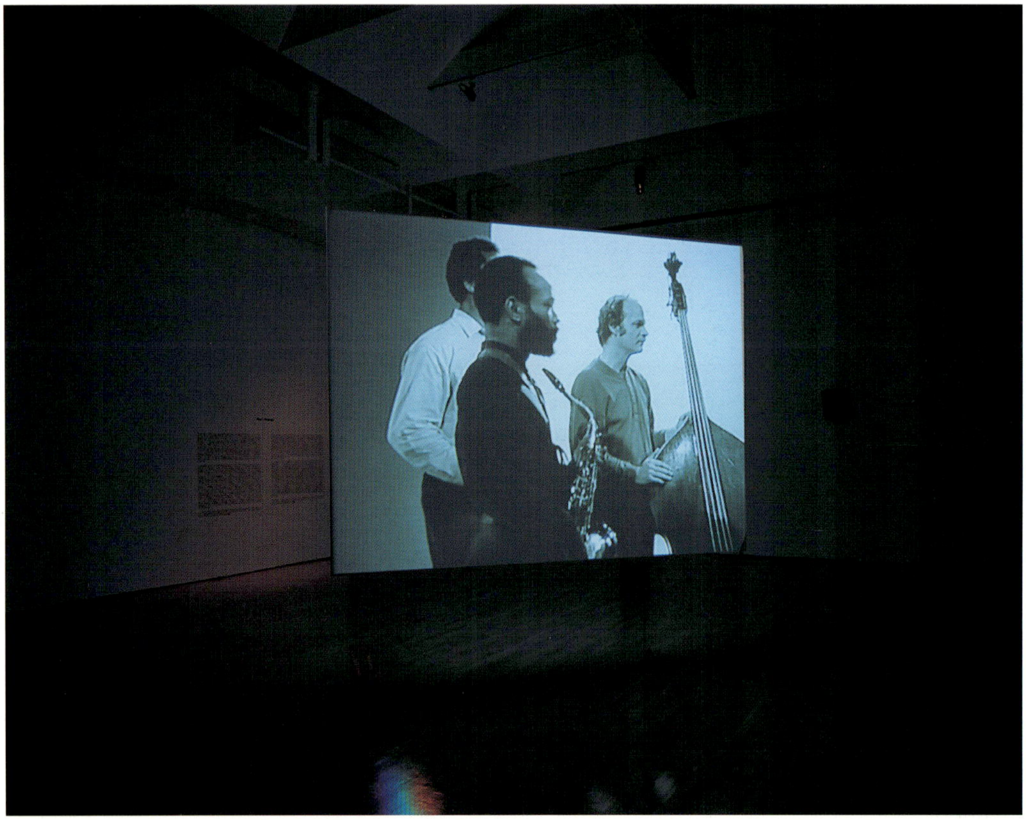

*Hors-champs*, 1992
Installation
Laserdisc projections on double-sided screen
Installation view at Musée d'art contemporain,
Montréal, 1996
Photo: Richard-Max Tremblay

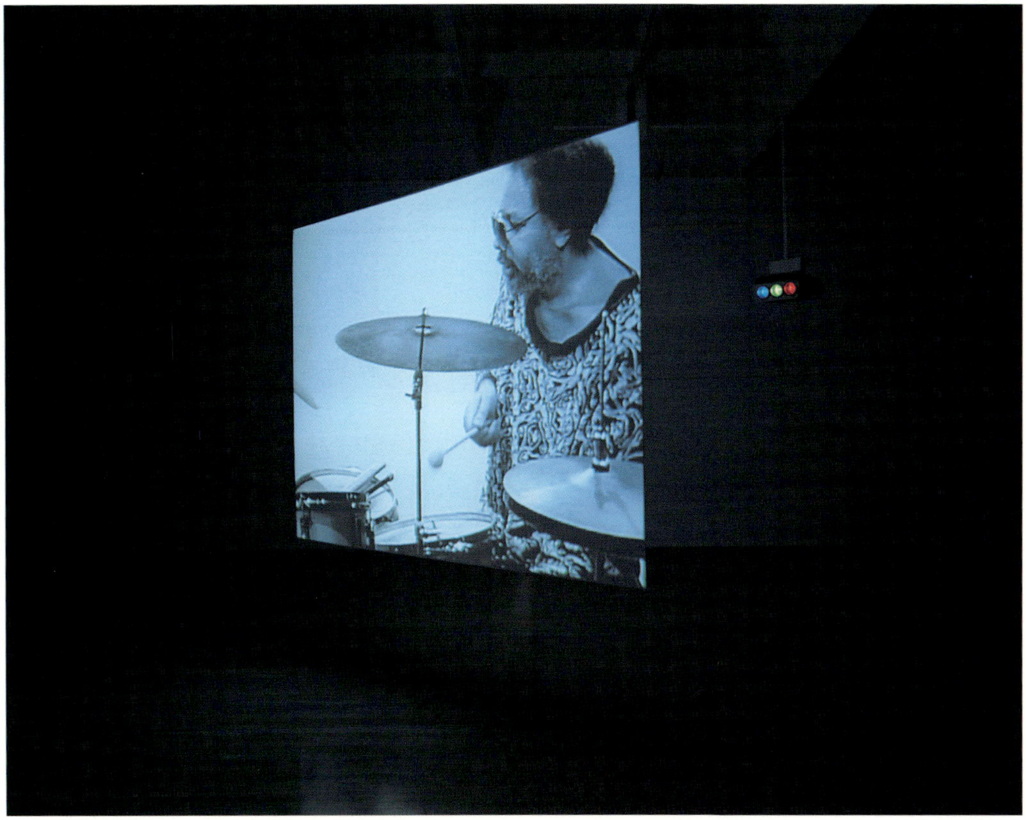

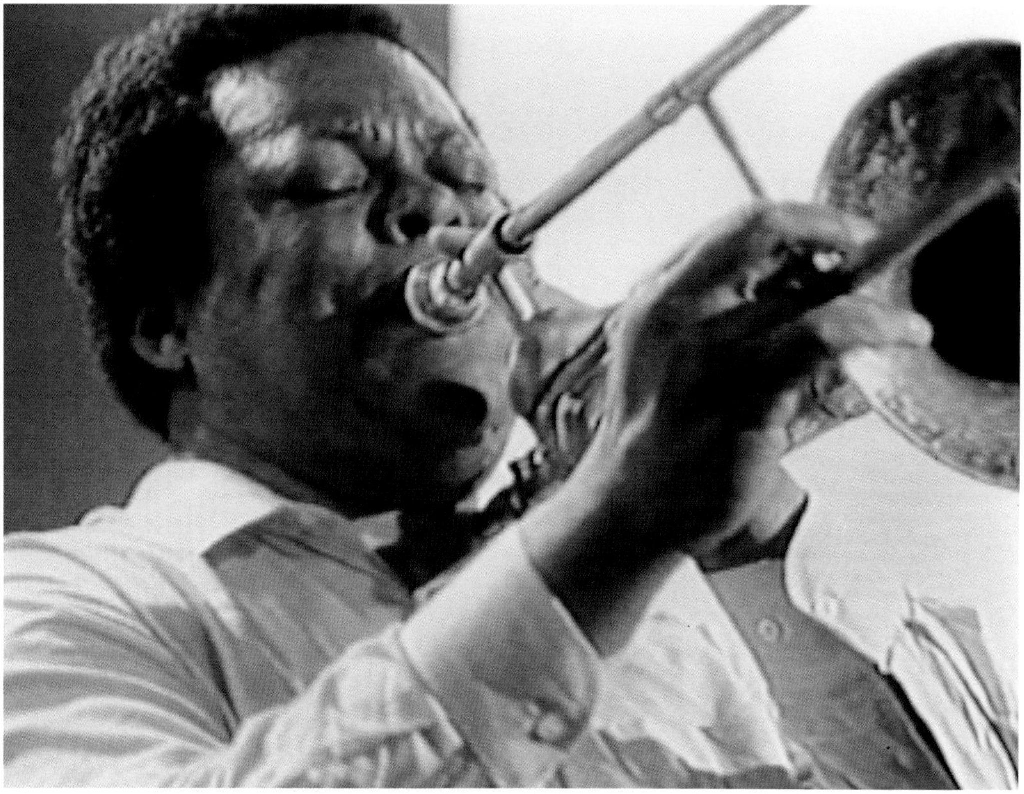

*Hors-champs*, 1992
Installation
Laserdisc projections on double-sided screen
Production still, Centre Georges Pompidou, Paris, 1992
Photo: Valérie Lagier

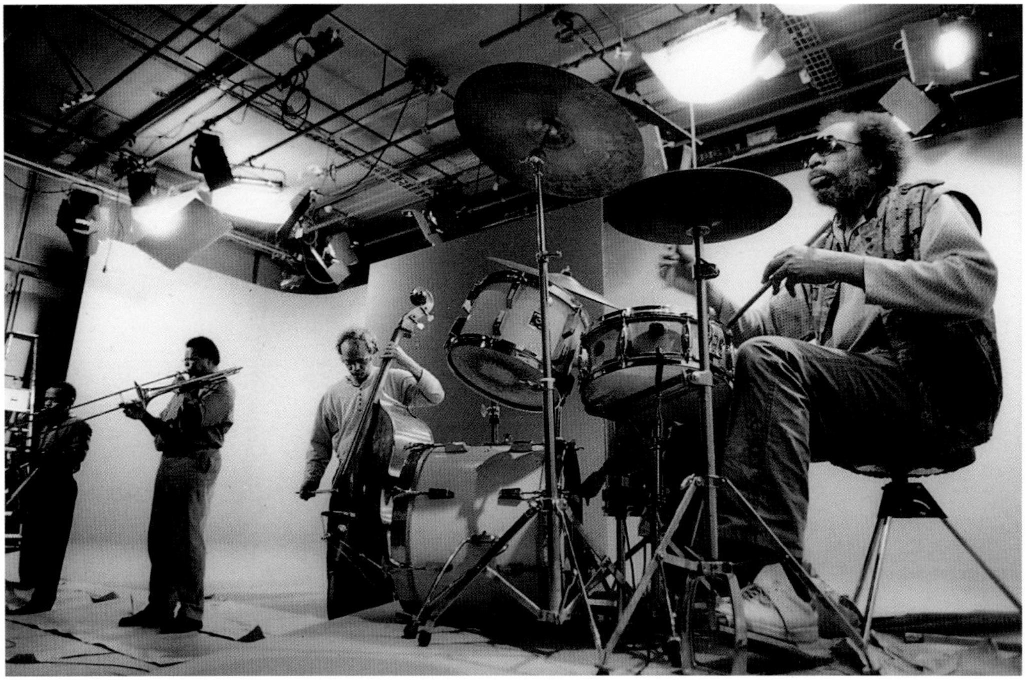

# WILLIAM FURLONG/ AUDIO ARTS

4
*Spoken For/Spoken About*, 1998
Recorded and constructed sound
The artist/Audio Arts

William Furlong was born in Surrey in 1944. He studied at Guildford School of Art from 1960 to 1965 and at the Royal Academy Schools from 1965 to 1968. In 1967 his work was included in the *New Contemporaries* at the Tate Gallery. In 1973 he founded *Audio Arts* magazine on cassette, and he presents his sound works under the name Audio Arts. Solo and group exhibitions include *Objects and Spaces* in *The Sculpture Show* at the Hayward Gallery in 1983 (in collaboration with Michael Archer), *Radio Garden* in the Tyne International Exhibition of Contemporary Art, 1990, *Absences/Presences* at the Ateliergemeinschaft, Münster in 1996, and *Life/Live* in Musée d'Art Moderne de la Ville de Paris in 1997. Among Audio Arts projects for 1998 are *Sound Garden*, commissioned by the Serpentine Gallery, and *An Imagery of Absence* for the Imperial War Museum, London. Furlong lives and works in London.

**What is the relationship between the distinct formats used to present the conversations you record and edit?**

The recorded voice acts as a material in my work. I am not particularly using the literal meanings in language but more precisely the linguistic 'fall out' between and around words. The recording process allows for repetition which facilitates a more focused 'auditory gaze' which as a result makes it possible to unlock the creative and expressive possibilities inherent within elements of aural sound. The work *Mute Dialogue*, 1997 is an example in which the 'uhms' and 'ahs', having been removed (as is usual from Audio Arts interviews over the last 18 months) were then re-used. In this work, these auditory equivalents outside of language were used to construct a work which implied meanings without the cultural, political and social underpinning of conventional language. The voice and its juxtapositions provide a rich opportunity to work with traces and the residue of meaning, through the verbal characteristic of emphasis, humour, accent, nationality, authority, vulnerability, gender, age, locality and so on. The time and space of the recording are also central considerations in the realisation of the work. Formats and procedures include collage, montage, rhythm, recycling, overlapping, repetition and accumulation.

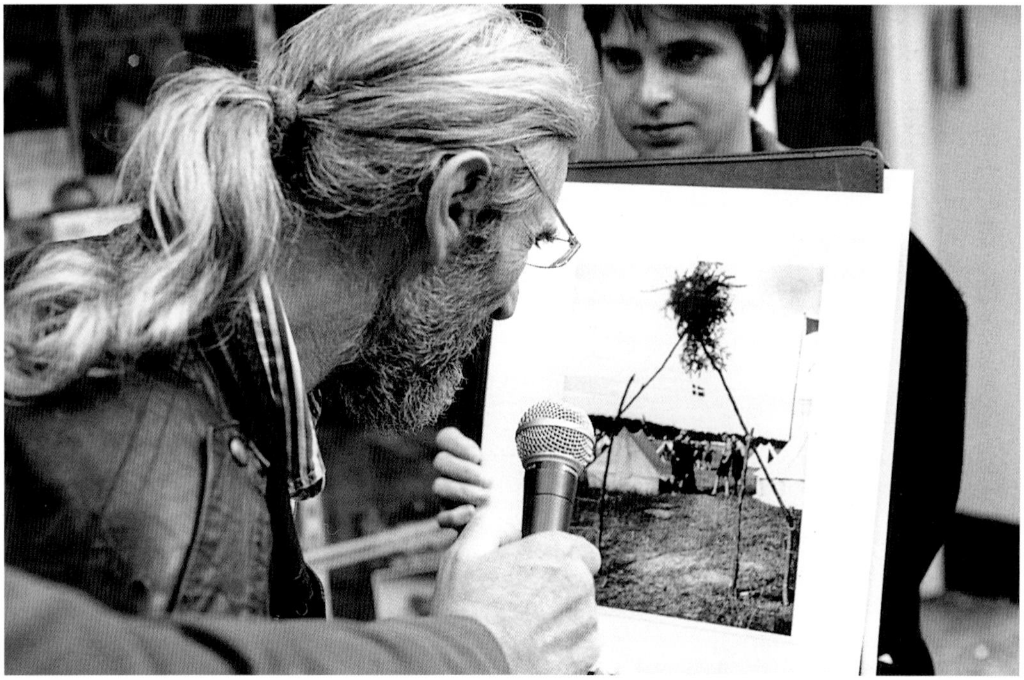

(above)
Gathering recorded material out on the streets for *An Imagery of Absence*, Imperial War Museum, 1998
Photo: Simon Day

(opposite)
*Absences/Presences*, 1996
Installation at Ateliergemeinschaft, Münster
Photo: Stephan Rache

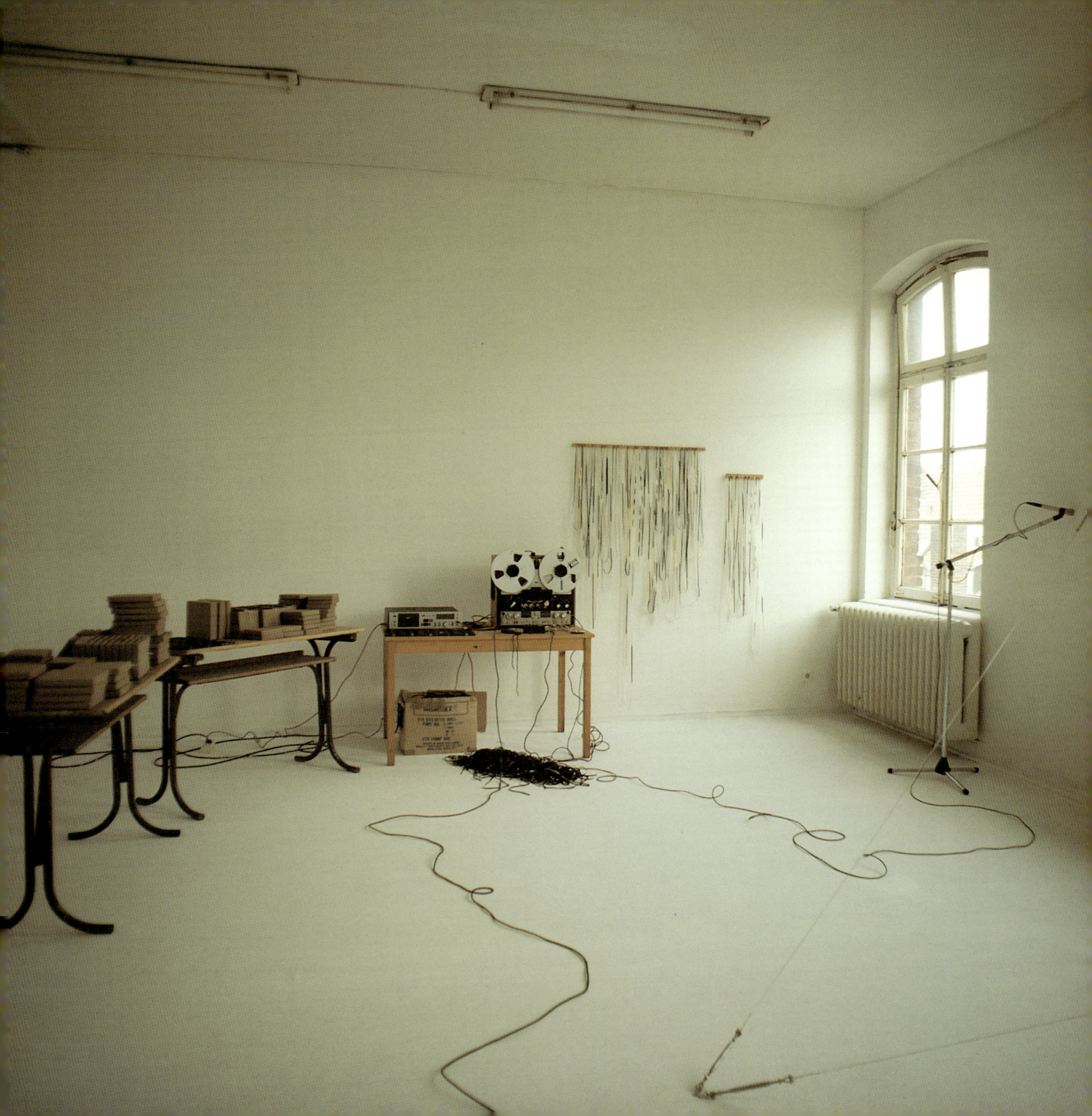

*Radio Garden*, 1990
Installation at Tyne International Exhibition
of Contemporary Art
Photo: William Furlong

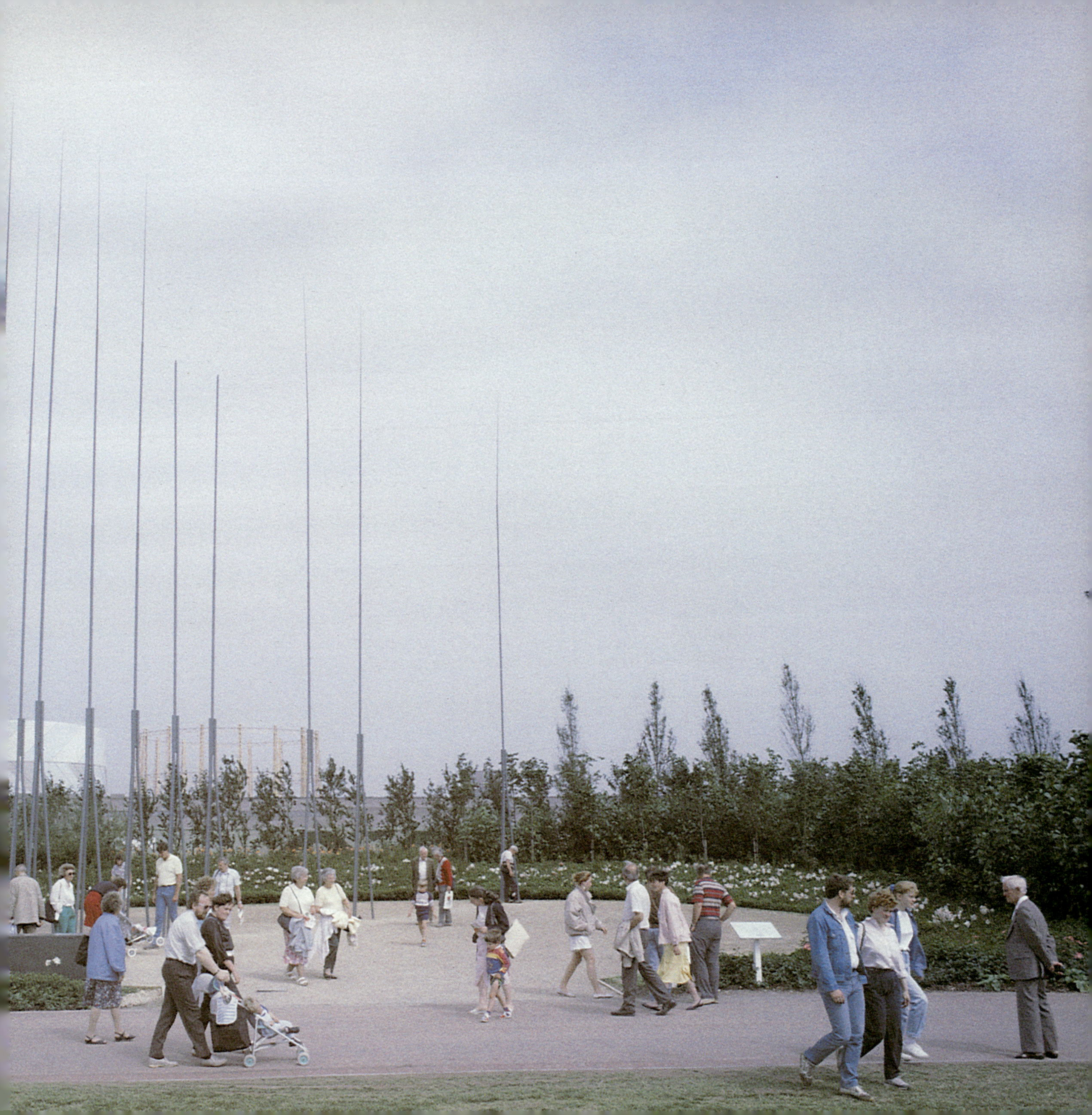

# JOSEPH GRIGELY

5
*Untitled Conversations and Portraits*, 1997-98
Mixed media
Dimensions variable
Courtesy of Air de Paris, Paris, and the artist

Joseph Grigely was born in 1956 in Springfield, Massachusetts, and was deafened in 1967 in the same town. He received his formal education at the National Technical Institute for the Deaf, Rochester from 1974 to 1975, at the New England College, West Sussex from 1976 to 1977, and at Oxford University from 1979 to 1984. His work was first exhibited in the *Summer Group Show* at the Blum Helman Warehouse, New York in 1992 and, in 1994, he had his two first solo exhibitions: *Conversations with the Hearing* at White Columns in New York and *Body Signs: Deviance, Difference, and Eugenics* in Washington DC. Grigely's work has been shown widely both in solo and group exhibitions in the USA and Europe, including *TransCulture* at the XLVI Venice Biennale in 1995, which then travelled to the Naoshima Museum of Contemporary Art in Naoshima, Japan, and the Istanbul Biennial in 1997. He lives and works in New York and Michigan.

**In what sense are your works intended to be heard?**

Oh, I don't know. I suppose someone might want to hear my stuff by forgetting what it's like to hear. Most of us are pretty much inured to our senses. This experience could be described as one of increasing familiarity, even indenturedness – day after day, year after year – we get so used to what it means to hear, or even what it means to see, that it's hard to break away from this. But that's what I want people to do – break away the familiar use of familiar senses, and spend some time experiencing little nothings. The Australian director Jocelyn Moorehouse made this astute film – it's called *Proof* – about a blind photographer who questions the validity of perception – and I like that immensely because it takes a position that the truth of our perceptions has so little to do with the truth of our imagination. The film seems to say: who cares what it means to have eyes or have ears – what matters is what we *do* with them. So the idea of getting lost in our senses – and taking pleasure in the process and not worrying if we're right or wrong – is very compelling for me. The fact that I'm deaf is pretty much an inescapable fact, but only in as much as it is an enabling rather than disabling condition. I like to imagine that it was like this for Beethoven too. A lot of people think it was unfortunate that he became deaf, but I don't. I think he was lucky – his deafness gave him another way of listening to the world.

*Paula H., New York, 24 May 1996*
R-print 1997
The artist

(overleaf)
*Untitled Conversation*, 1996
Ink on paper
The artist

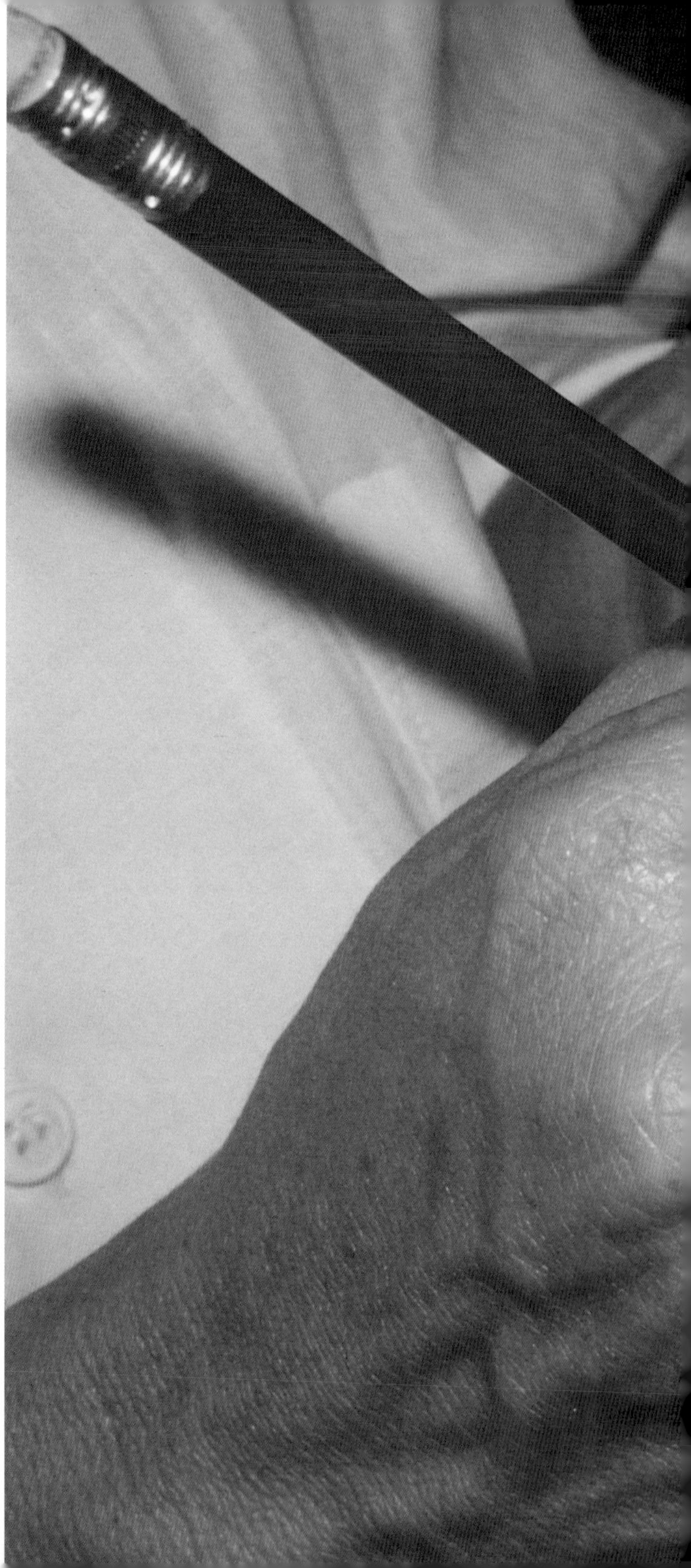

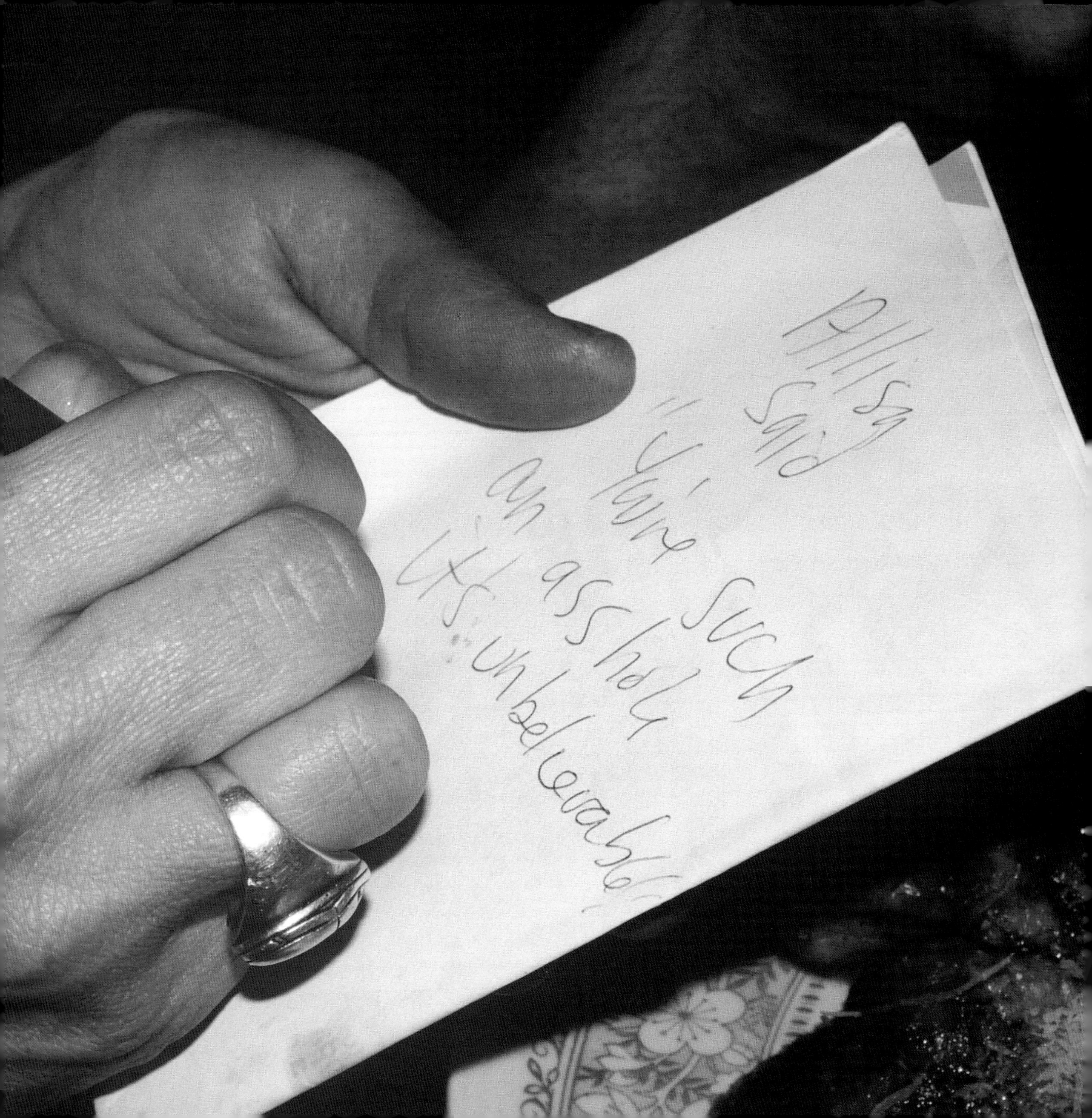
Millsy
says
you're such
an asshole
it's unbelievable

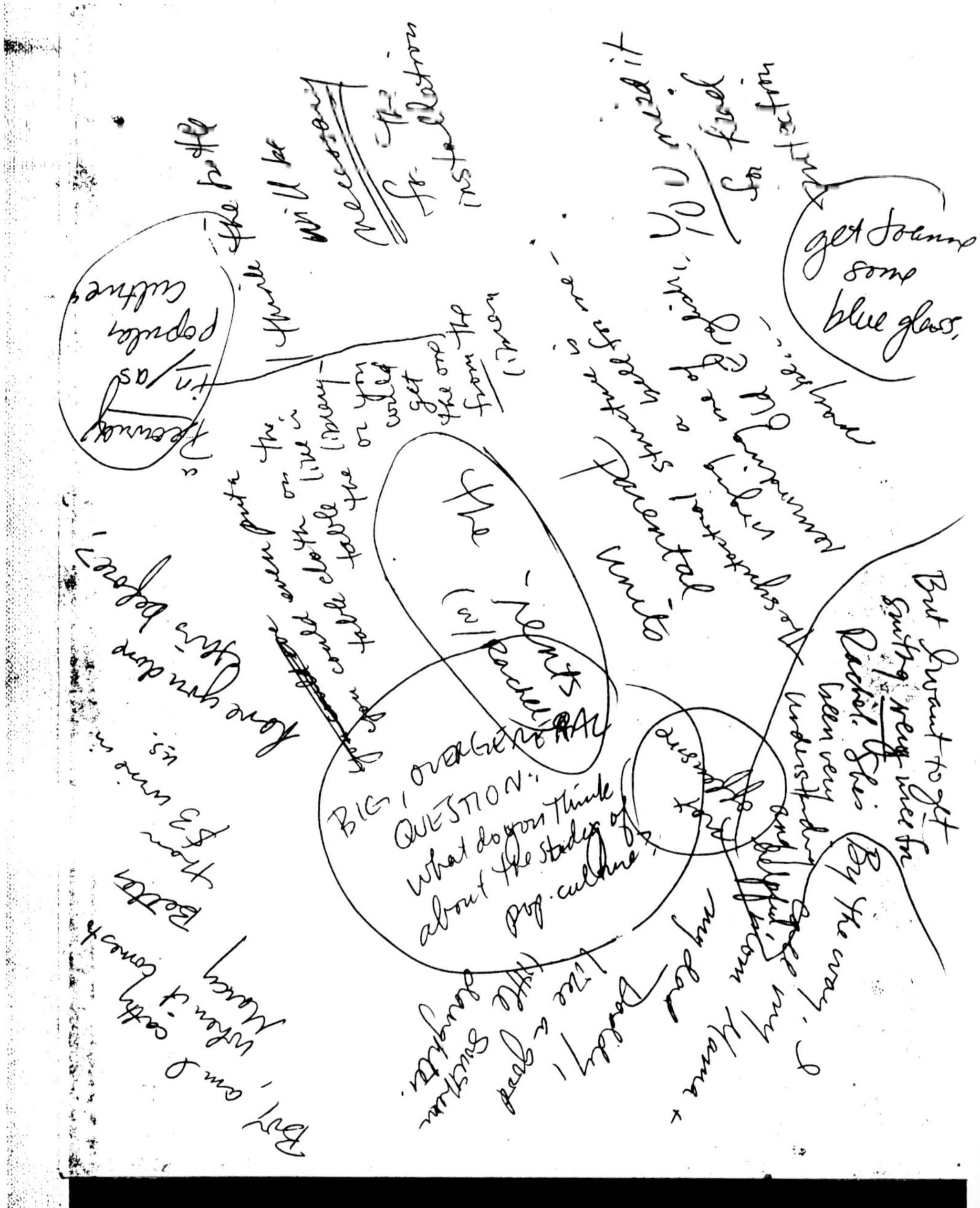

get Joanne some blue glass;
YOU need it for fund-raiser...
Deconstructing is like a biker babe or some Old Symbol...
Parental units
The 'rents (w/ Rachel)
BIG, OVERGENERAL QUESTION: what do you think about the study of pop. culture?
But I want to get something very nice for Rachel. She's been very understanding and helpful.
By the way, I call my Mom Mama + my dad Daddy, like a good little Southern daughter.
Have you done this before?
Will be necessary for the installation
think the bottle is Recovery
popular culture
Bet, can I catch some of what is money
Better than $3 wine in us.

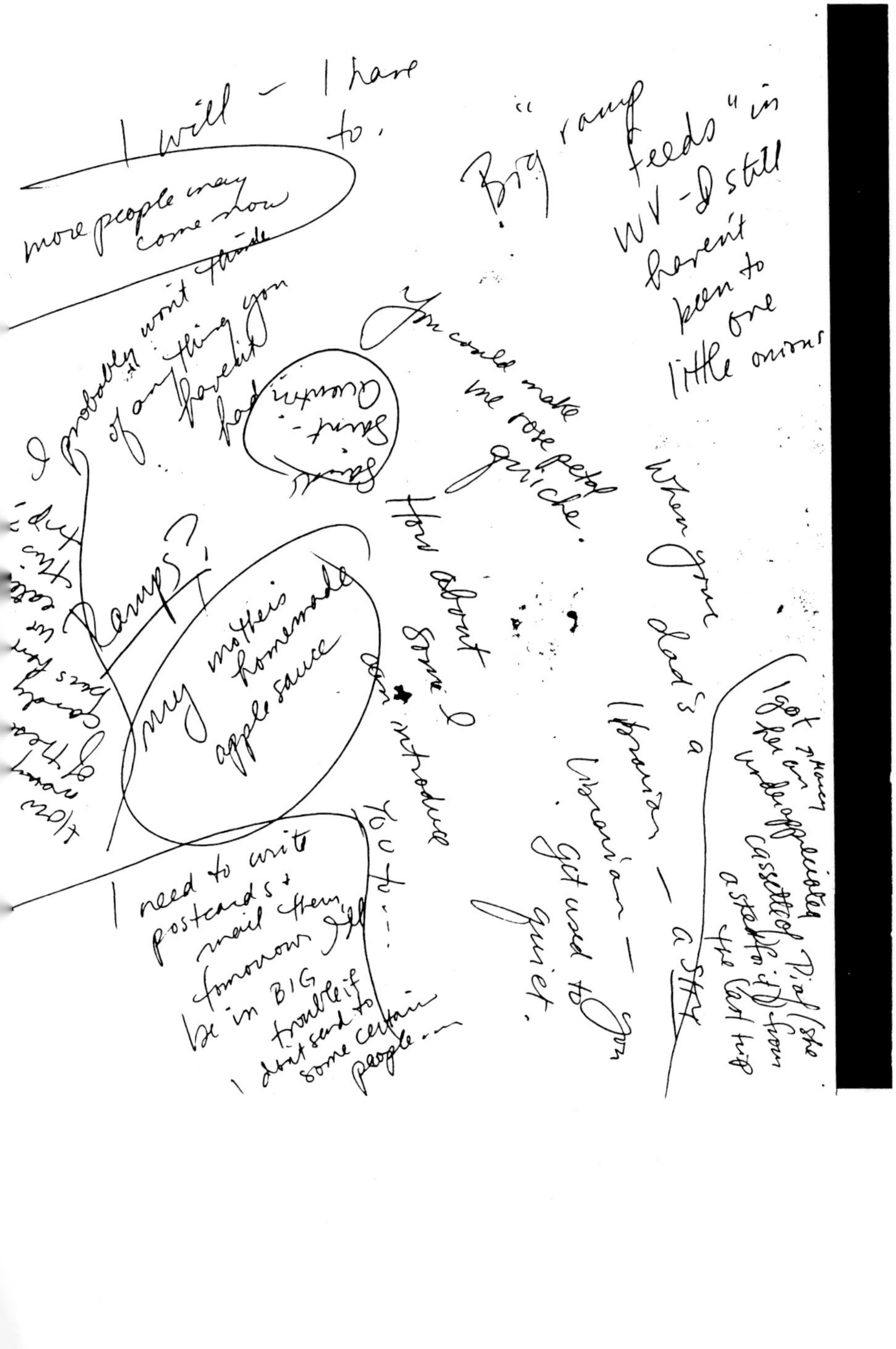
I will — I have to.
more people may come now
I probably won't think of anything you haven't had
Saint Quentin
Ramps?
my mother's homemade apple sauce
You could make me rose petal quiche.
How about some I can introduce YOU to...
"Big ramp feeds" in WV - I still haven't been to one
little onions
When your dad's a librarian — a SPY
librarian — you get used to quiet.
I got her an underappreciated cassette of Piaf (she asked for it) from the last trip
I need to write postcards + mail them tomorrow I'll be in BIG trouble if I don't send to some certain people...

# LUCY GUNNING

6
*The Singing Lesson*, 1994
Video installation with 2 monitors
(duration 60 minutes)
Courtesy Matt's Gallery

Lucy Gunning was born in Newcastle upon Tyne in 1964. In 1984 she studied for a Diploma in Foundation Studies at West Surrey College of Art and Design before enrolling at Falmouth School of Art in 1987 and Goldsmiths College in 1994. Her first solo exhibition took place at the Adam Gallery, London, in 1995, followed by solo exhibitions in Boston, Preston, New York, and most recently at Matt's Gallery, London. Since 1987 Gunning's work has been included in over 30 group shows in numerous European cities as well as in the USA, Mexico and Japan. She received the BT New Contemporaries Award in 1994. She lives and works in London.

**Your work focuses on the struggle to articulate using different languages or modes of expression. Why?**

I don't think my work in general does 'focus' on the struggle to articulate. However, two works do have some relevance to your question. Certainly in *Malcolm, Lloyd, Angela, Norman, Jane*, 1997 (Matt's Gallery) the subjects represented on the monitors have varying degrees of aberrations in their speech. They're specifically chosen to emphasize the mechanisms of speech and to defamiliarise one's relationship to language — highlighting amongst other things the potentially anarchic relationship the voice/body has towards language. In *The Singing Lesson*, 1994 there is an acknowledgement of what a remarkable thing the voice is: air passing through the body shaped by a muscle in the throat; how it comes from an inside to an outside and yet is neither; what one has to do with one's body to make a certain sound. There is an interest in the relationship between the trained and the untrained voice. The notion of the Lesson is encountered with all the desire, shame, vulnerability, humour, growth and 'struggle' explicit in the learning process, which is somehow twofold in the process of learning to sing.

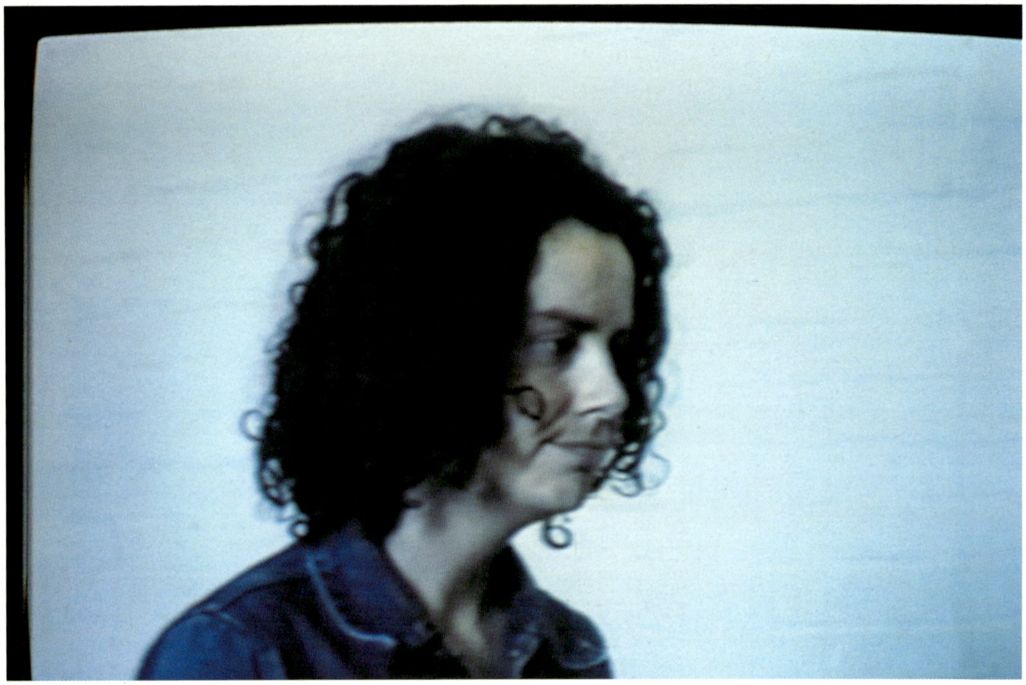

*The Singing Lesson*, 1994
(details above and opposite; installation shot below opposite)
Video installation with 2 monitors
(duration 60 minutes)
Courtesy Matt's Gallery
Photo: Lucy Gunning

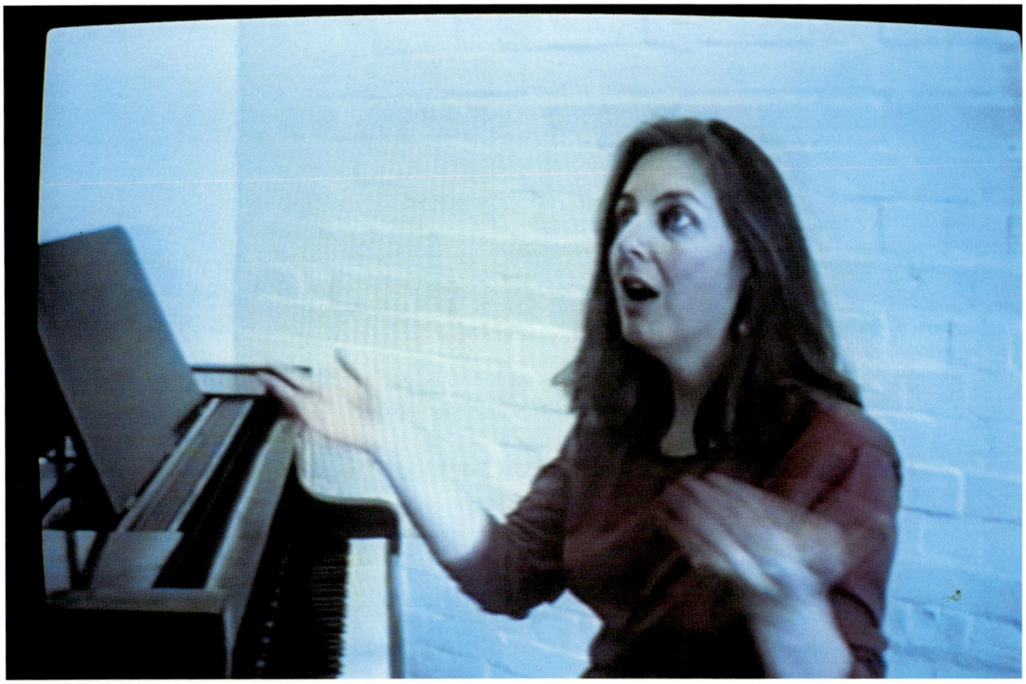

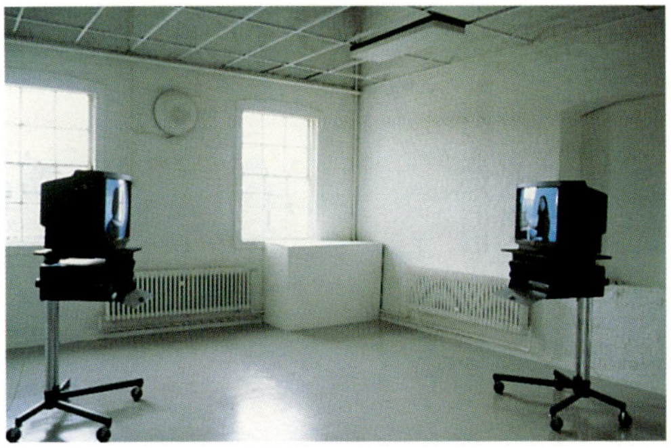

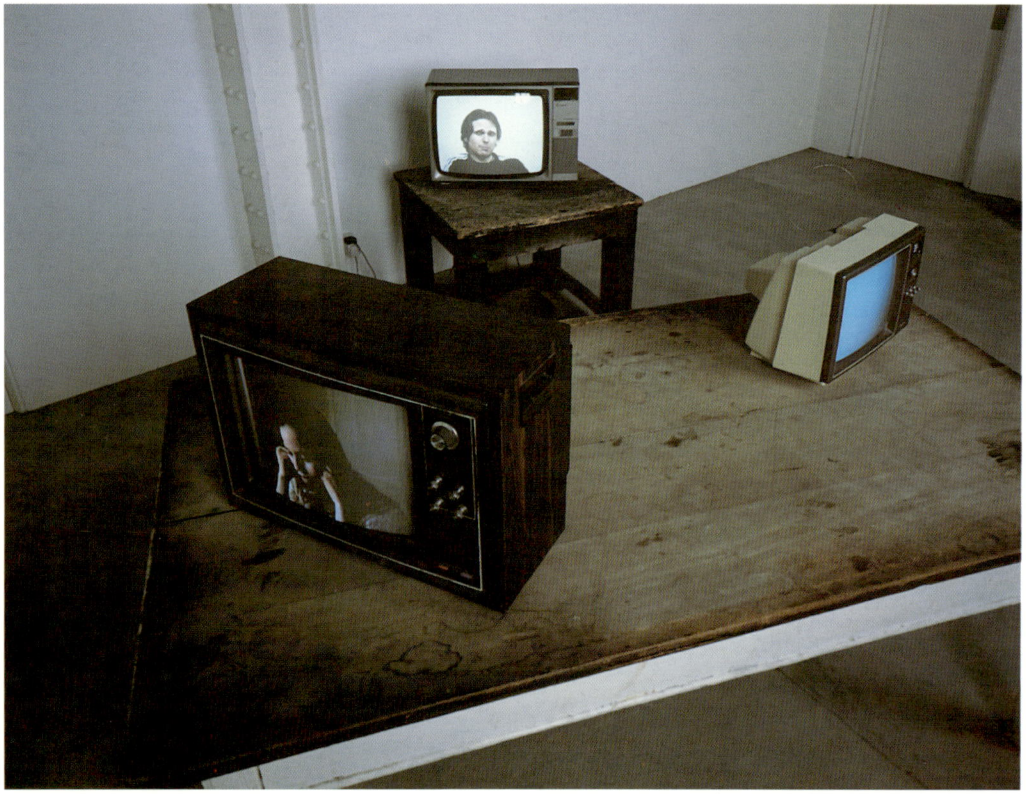

(above and opposite)
*Malcolm, Lloyd, Angela, Norman, Jane* 1997
two details from the installation at Matt's Gallery
5 monitors, tables and staircase; video with sound
(duration 18 minutes)
Courtesy Matt's Gallery
Photo: Stephen White

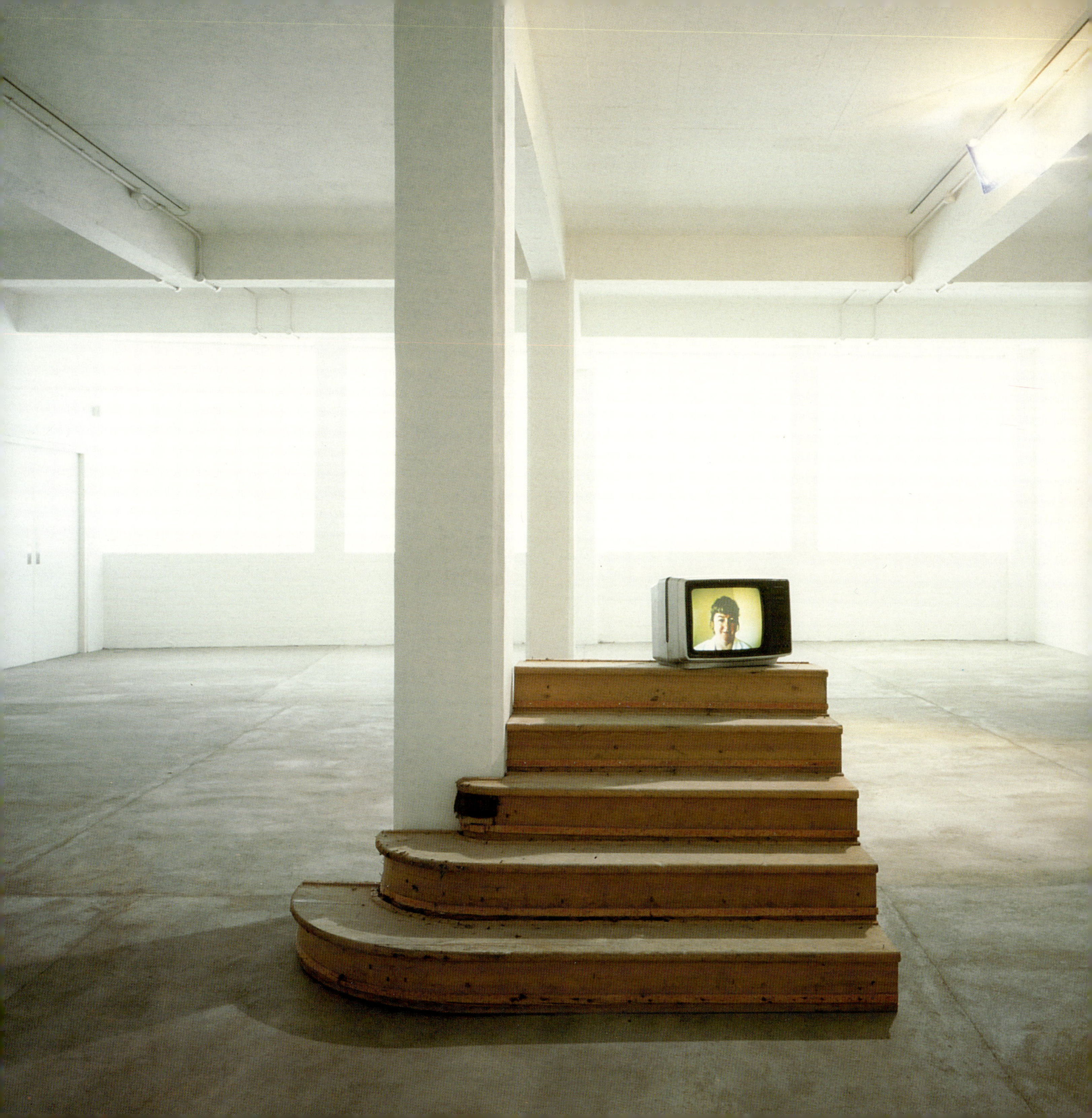

# BETHAN HUWS

7
*Singing for the Sea*, 1993
16mm Standart, colour, optic sound
(duration 12 minutes plus credits)
The artist


Bethan Huws was born in Bangor, Wales, in 1961. She studied at Middlesex Polytechnic from 1981 to 1985, and at the Royal College of Art, London, from 1986 to 1988. Her first solo exhibition was at the Riverside Studios, London, in the summer of 1989. Subsequently she has exhibited at the Kunsthalle, Bern, the ICA, London, and the Museum Haus Esters in Krefeld. In 1993 Artangel, London, commissioned her to make *The Bistritsa Babi – A Work for the North Sea*, which took place near Alnwick, Northumbria, on 22, 23 and 24 July. Her work has been included in *The British Art Show* in 1990, *Life/Live* in 1997 at the Musée d'Art Moderne de la Ville de Paris, and *Sculpture. Projects in Münster* in 1997. She lives and works in Malakoff, France.

**Who is singing, and to whom, in your work *Singing for the Sea*, 1993?**

A group of eight extraordinary Bulgarian women singing to all existence.

To a thing.

a phenomenon.

a happening.

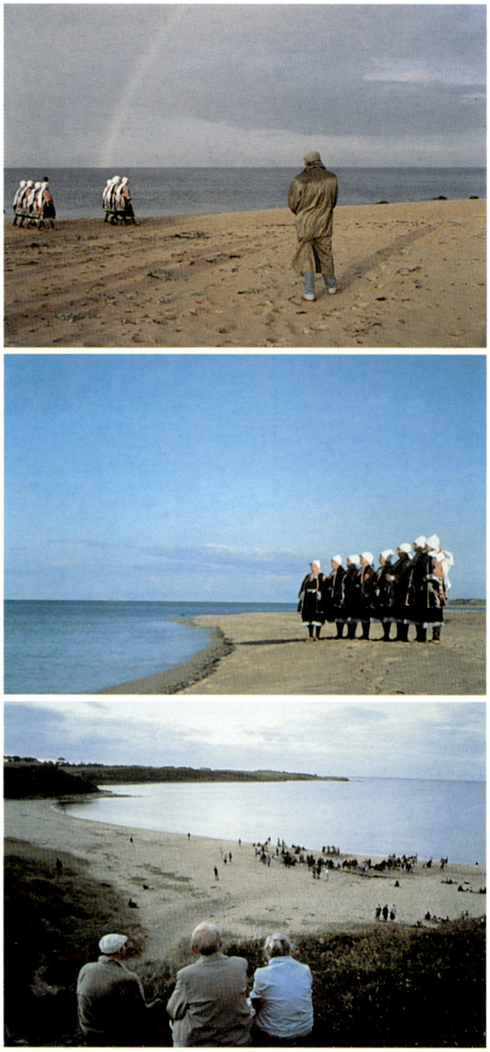

*The Bistritsa Babi - A Work for the North Sea*,
July 1993 (three details)
Performance
Commissioned by Artangel
© ADAGP, Paris and DACS, London 1998
Photo: I. Jedrzigczyk

**Who is singing, and to whom, in your work *Singing for the Sea*, 1993?**

A group of eight extraordinary Bulgarian women singing to all existence.
To a thing.
a phenomenon.
a happening.

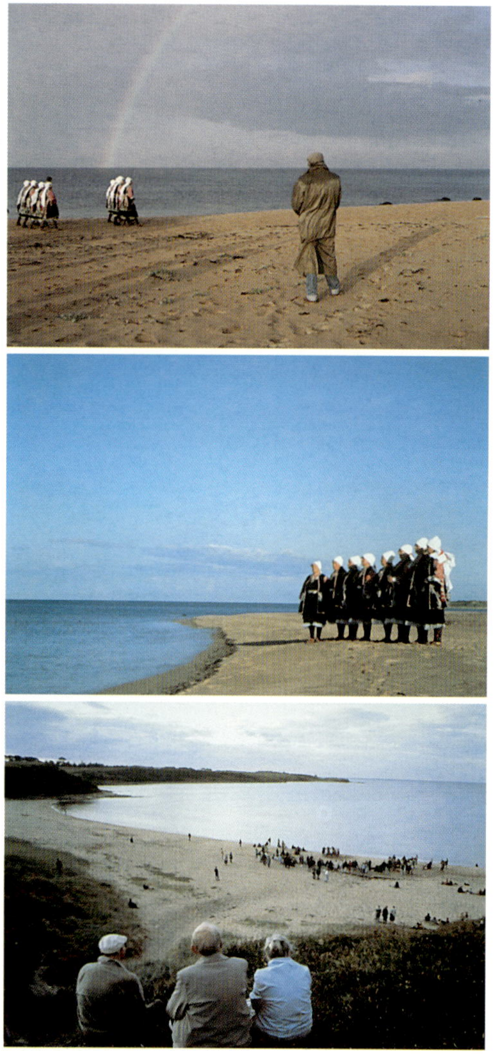

*The Bistritsa Babi - A Work for the North Sea*,
July 1993 (three details)
Performance
Commissioned by Artangel

Photo: I. Jedrzigczyk

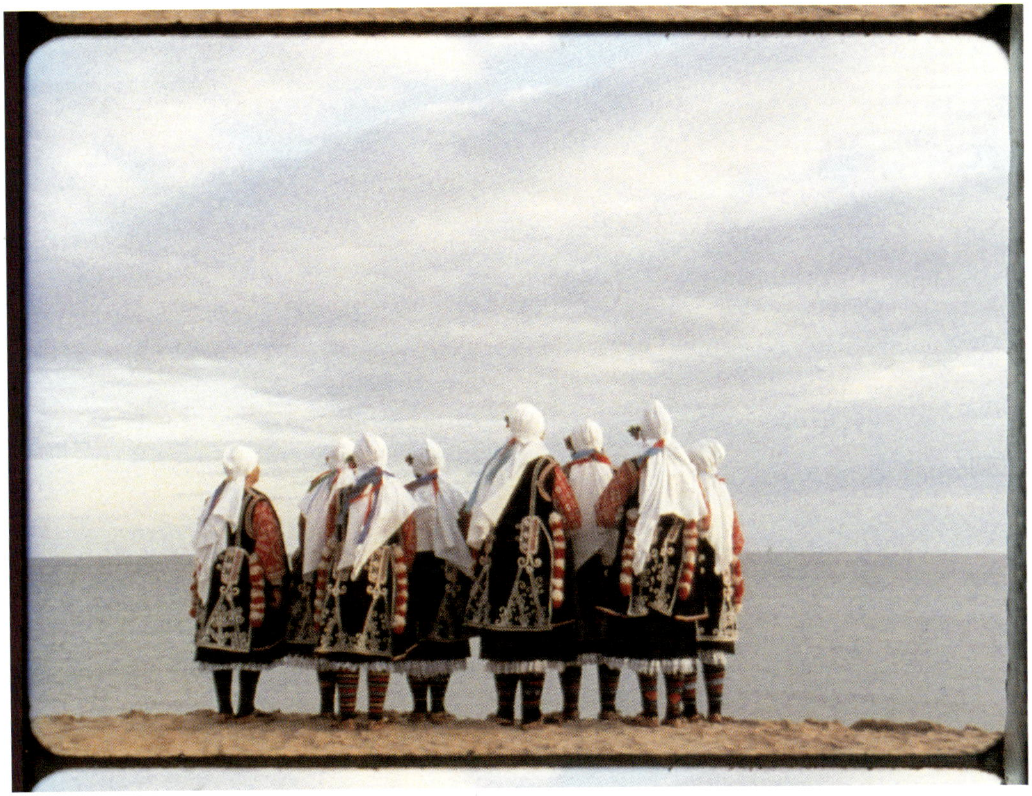



(above and overleaf)
*Singing for the Sea*, 1993 (detail)
16 mm Standart, colour, optic sound
(duration 12 minutes plus credits)

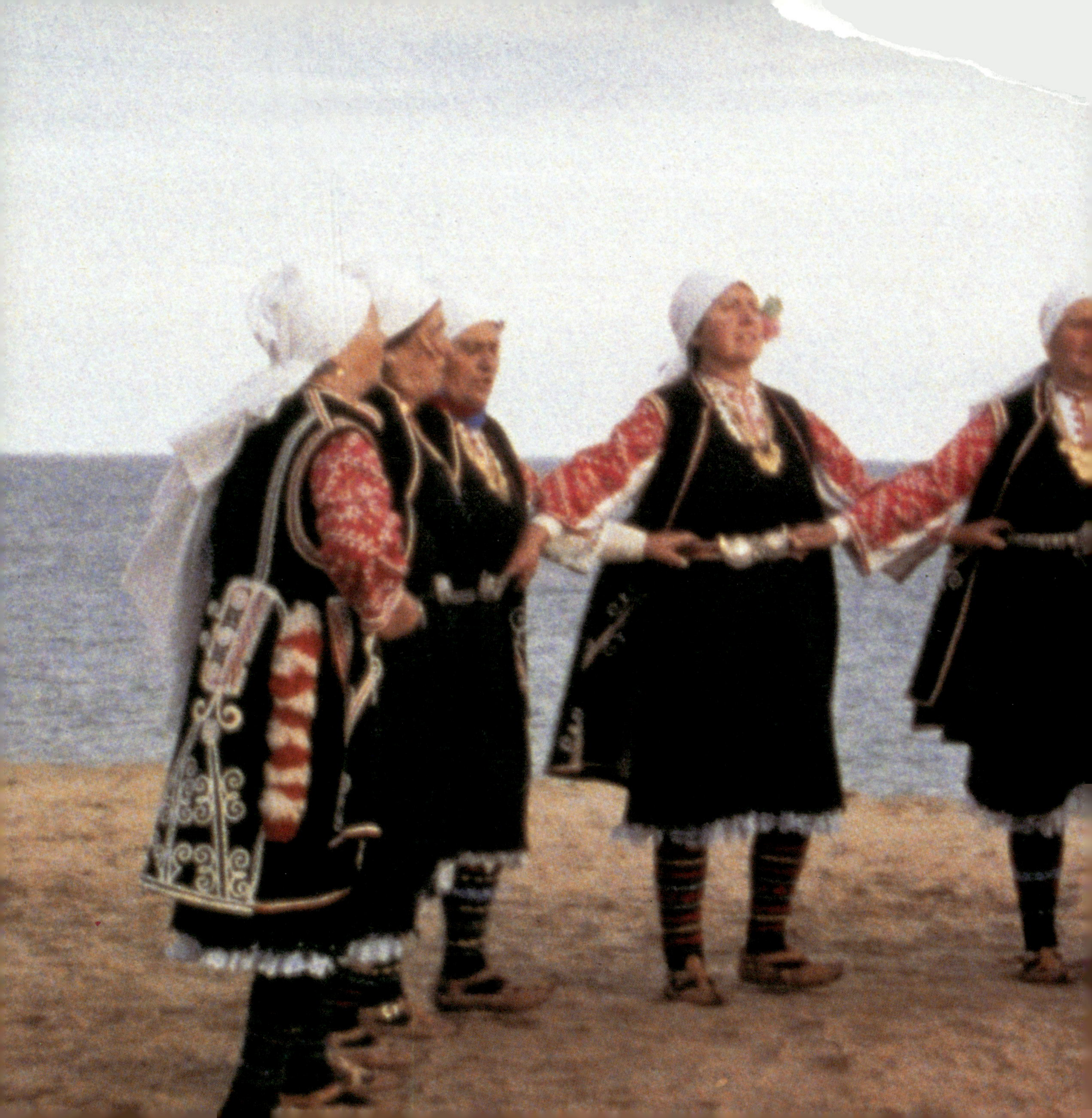

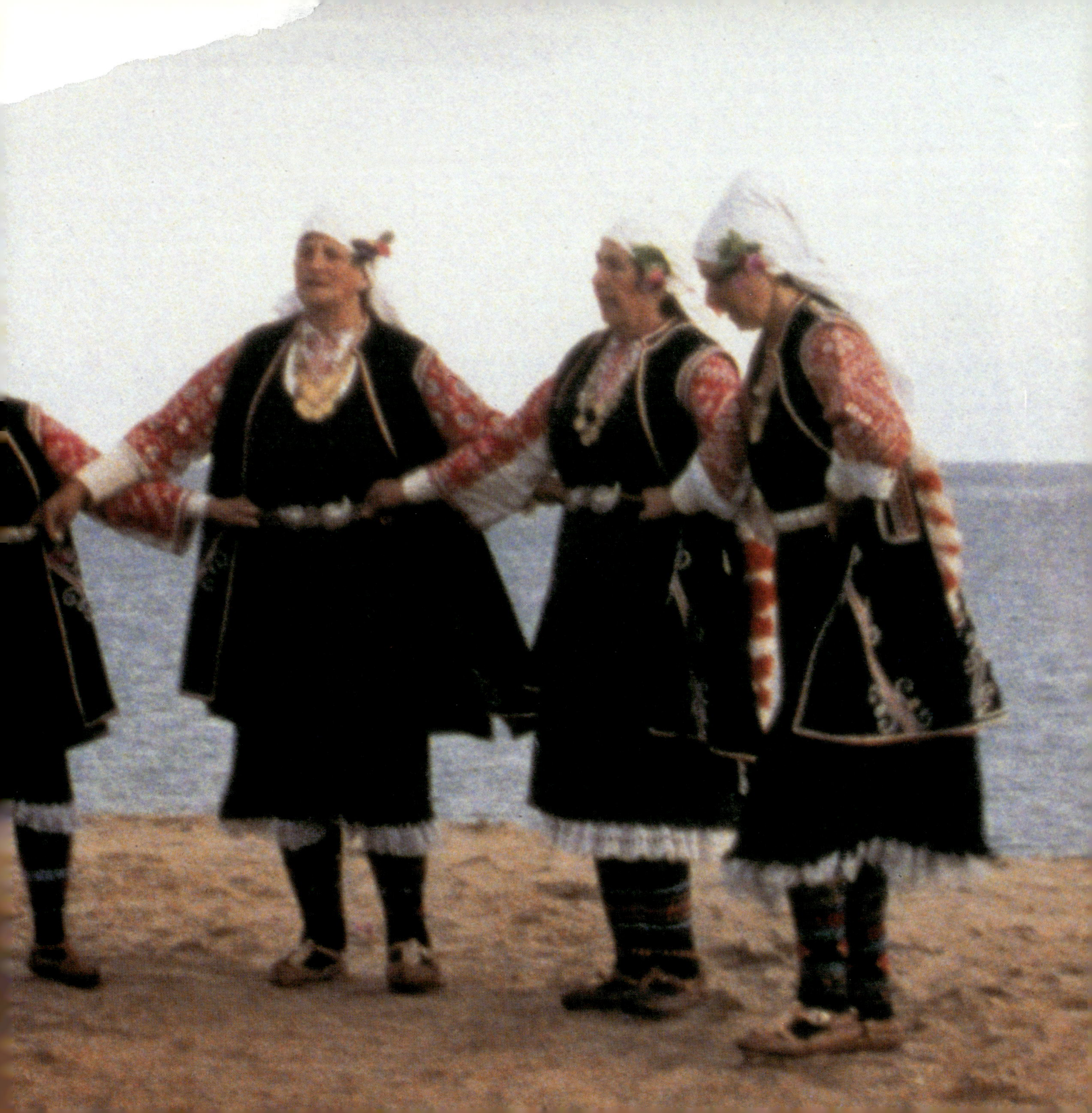

# JUAN MUÑOZ

8
*Ventriloquist Looking at a Double Interior*, 1988
Papier mâché, chalk on canvas
Dimensions variable
The Carol and Arthur Goldberg Collection

Juan Muñoz was born in Madrid in 1953. He attended the Central School of Art and Design, London from 1976 to 1977, Croydon College of Design and Technology, London from 1979 to 1980, and Pratt Graphic Center, New York in 1982. Muñoz had his first solo exhibition in 1984 at the Galeria Fernando Vijande in Madrid. Major solo shows include those at Arnolfini Gallery, Bristol, 1990, the Irish Museum of Modern Art, Dublin, 1994, The Museo Nacional Centro de Arte Reina Sofía, Madrid, 1996, and *A Place Called Abroad* at the Dia Center for the Arts, New York, 1997. He has participated in numerous group exhibitions including *Possible Worlds* at the ICA, London in 1990, and the Carnegie International in Pittsburg in 1991. He lives and works in Madrid.

**Your work strongly evokes, but does not actually incorporate, sound in general and the voice in particular. What kind of conversations do you imagine pass between your figures?**

Sitting at my desk, right now, as I write, I try to imagine that other moment when a ventriloquist sits down to rehearse with the doll in the dressing-room or at home. I try to imagine that very moment when he utters the first word, the first sentence. One has the tongue, the other the language.

Of all the feelings I know, perhaps the one that seems to me the most profound is bewilderment. I imagine that for a ventriloquist, or for the chatty doll, bewilderment must be the moment in which, at the beginning of the rehearsal, they greet each other.

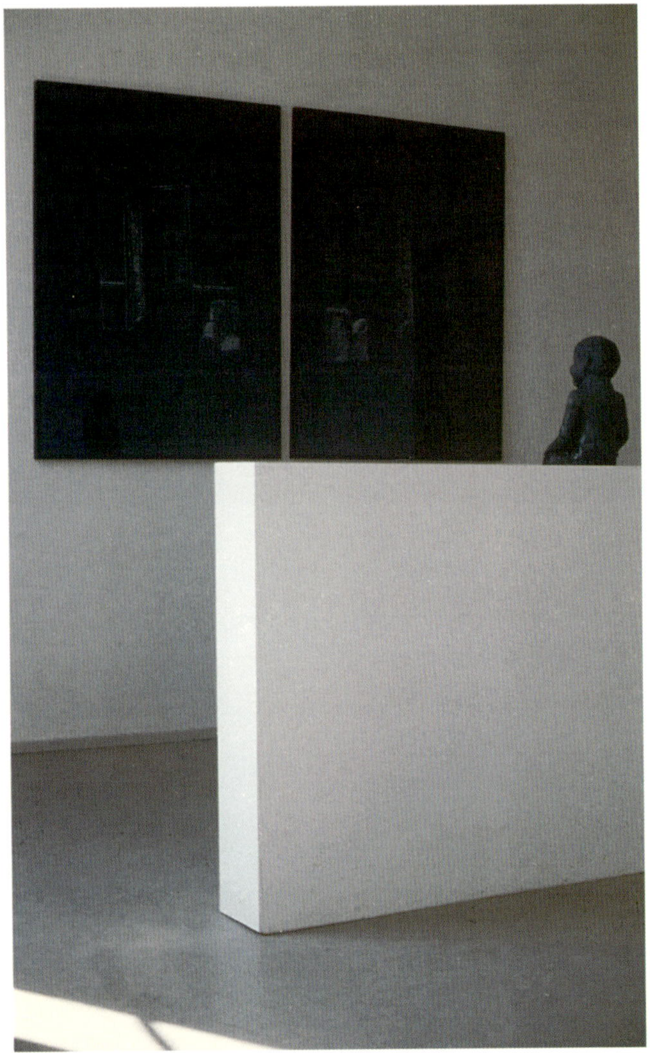

(above)
*Ventriloquist Looking at a Double Interior*, 1988
Papier mâché, chalk on canvas
Dimensions variable
The Carol and Arthur Goldberg Collection

(opposite)
*Neal's Last Words*, 1997
Resin, silicone, motor, mirror
140 x 50 x 50 cm
Photo: Galleria Continua, San Gimignano (Si), Italy

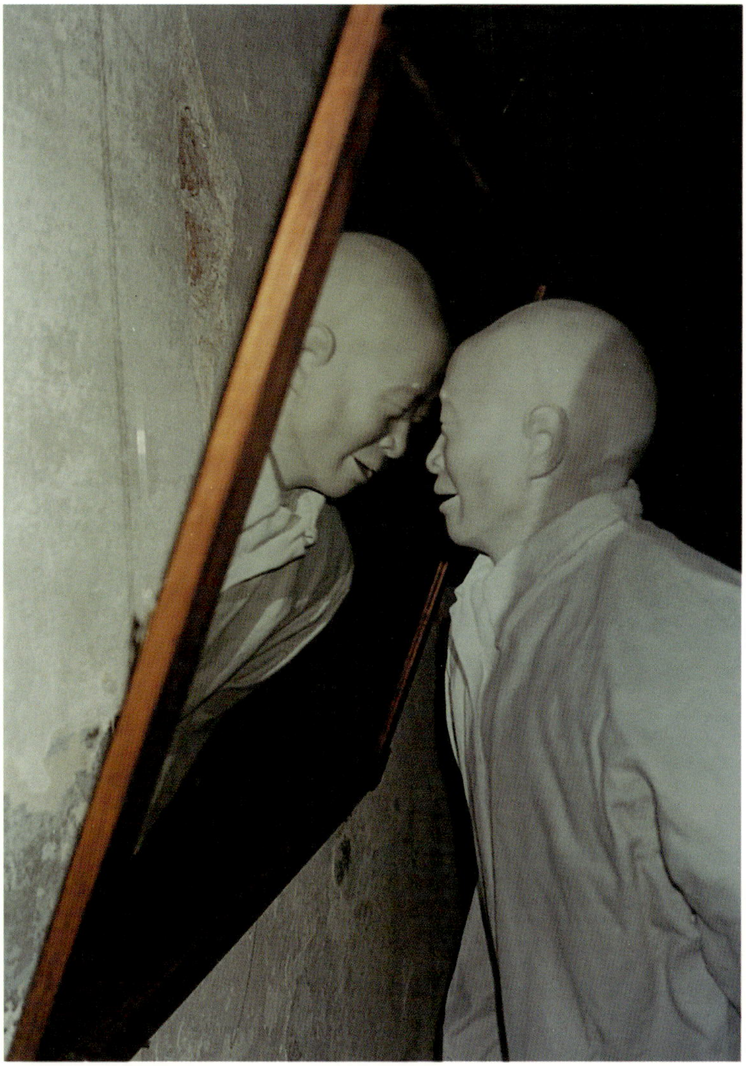

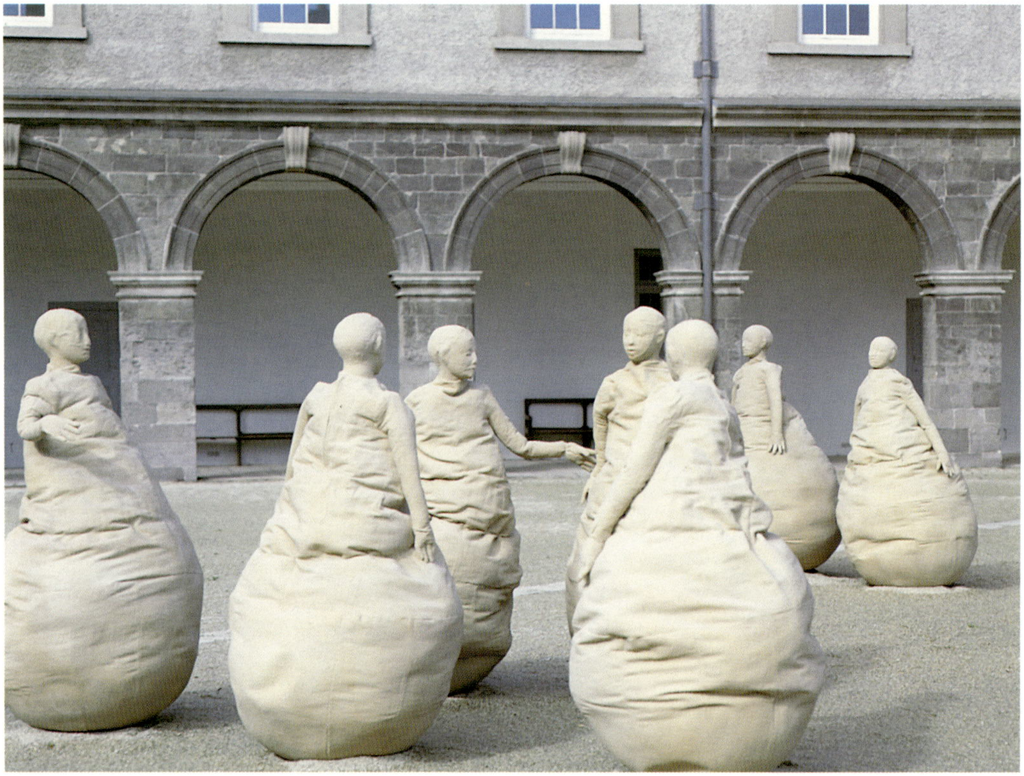

(above)
*Conversation Piece (Dublin)*, 1994 (detail)
Resin, sand, cloth
140 x 70 x 70 each figure
The artist
Photo: Kristien Daem

(opposite)
*The Prompter*, 1988
Iron, papier mâché, bronze and wood
Dimensions variable
The artist
Photo: Peter Cox

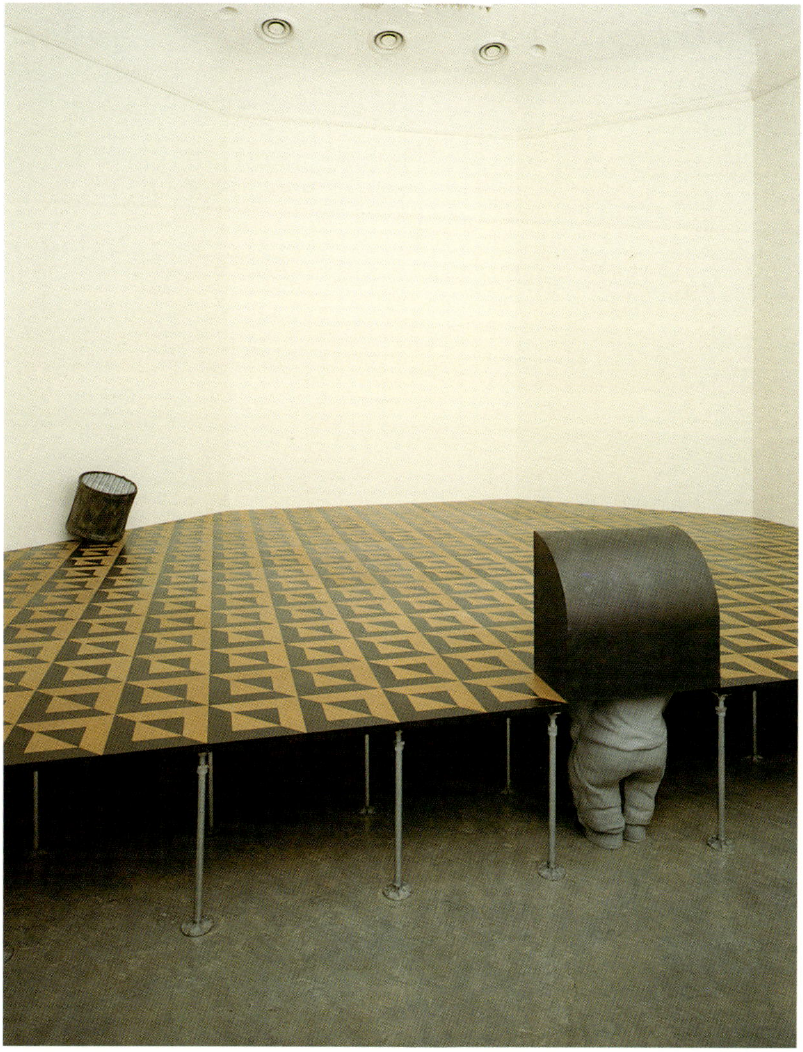

# ROSS SINCLAIR

9
*Dead Church/Real Life*, 1998
Installation
The artist

Ross Sinclair was born in Glasgow in 1966. He attended Glasgow School of Art (Environmental Art Department) between 1984 and 1990, and completed his Masters in Fine Arts there in 1992; he also attended California Institute of the Arts in 1992. *Fan Club* at the Stills Gallery, Edinburgh, in 1991 was his first solo exhibition and he has continued to exhibit regularly. In 1996 the CCA, Glasgow mounted *Real Life Rocky Mountain*, and in 1997 he had a solo show at Mercer Union, Toronto. He has exhibited in numerous group exhibitions in Europe and America, notably *Glasgow* at the Kunsthalle Bern in 1997. Since 1995 Sinclair has been a part-time lecturer at Glasgow School of Art (Environmental Art Department). He lives and works in Glasgow.

### What is folk music?

Folk music is the first song you play when you get up in the morning and it's the last one you play before you go out at night. Other people might say they can't understand it but it sure as hell makes sense to you. It's the tune you play majestically, top volume at 3am and fuck the neighbours. The passion of this music makes life worth living.* And the power of this music will make you wonder if Art could ever be as good.

*I have never believed in God. So I was perturbed when I found out that songs like *Abide With Me* and *How Great Thou Art* could make me cry. They seem so perfect, these hymns. They have all the answers. They make everything fit together, make sense. On the few occasions I've been in church I've never allowed myself to sing them, although I really wanted to. But how could I – they are the antitheses of everything I believe. Well, I'm going to sing them for you now. I wonder what will happen? They say the devil has all the best tunes... let's find out.

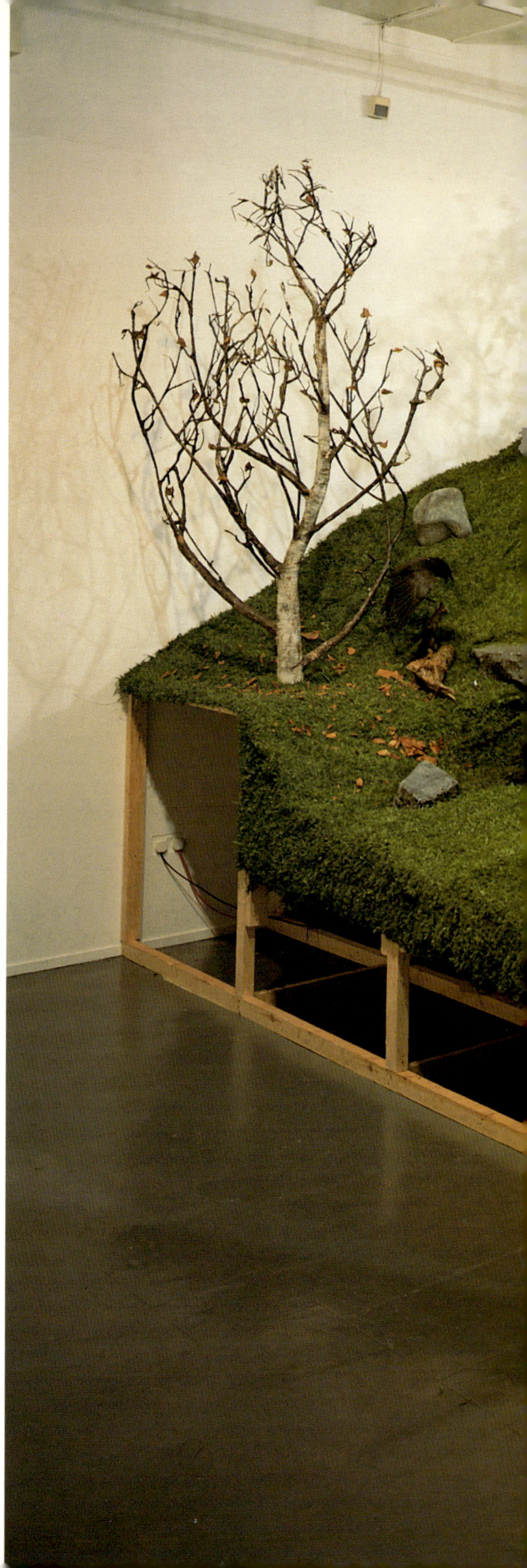

*Real Life Rocky Mountain*, 1996
Installation at CCA, Glasgow
Photo: Simon Starling

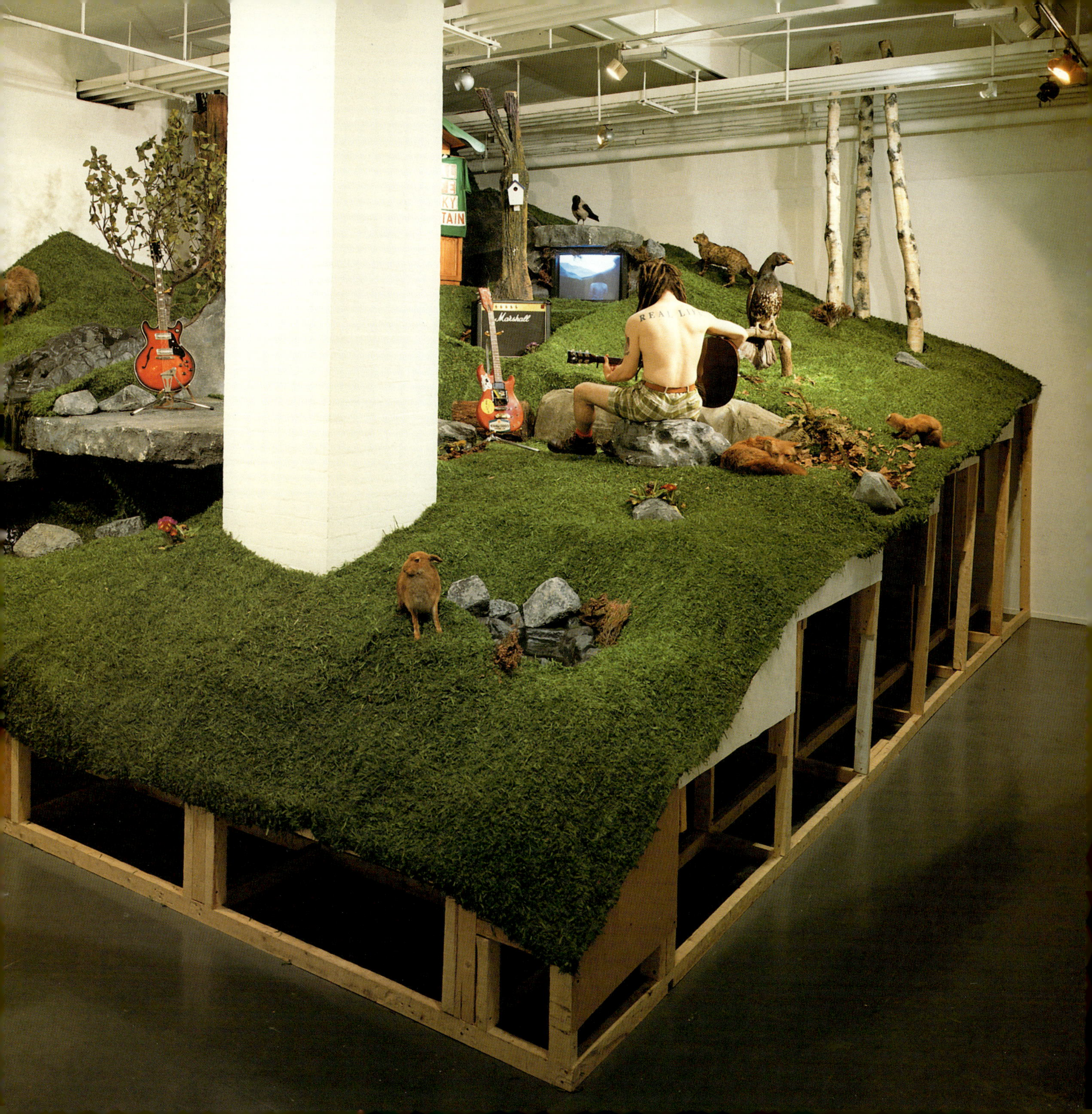
Marshall

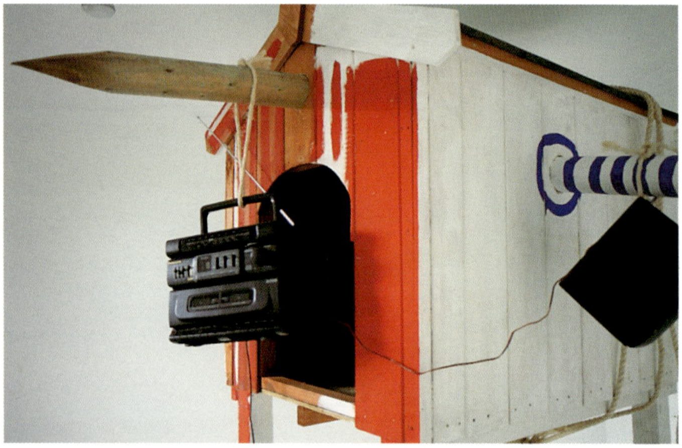

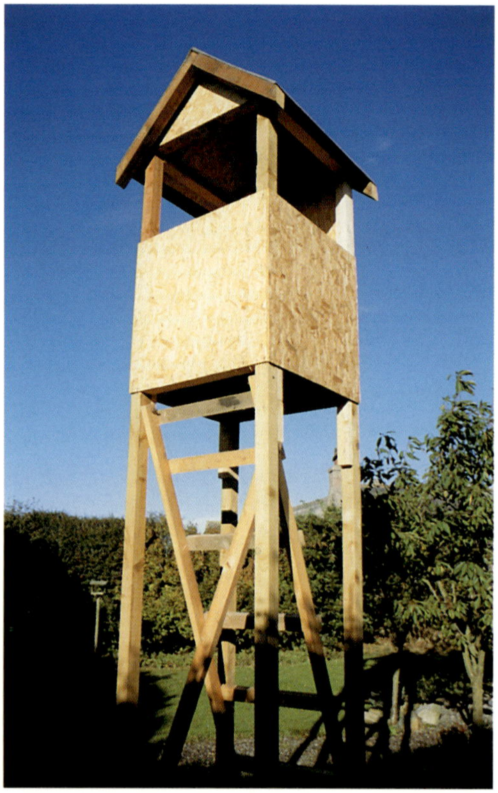



*I, Messiah, Am Jailer*, 1997 (two details)
Iain Irving Gallery, Aberdeenshire
Installation
Photo: Iain Irving

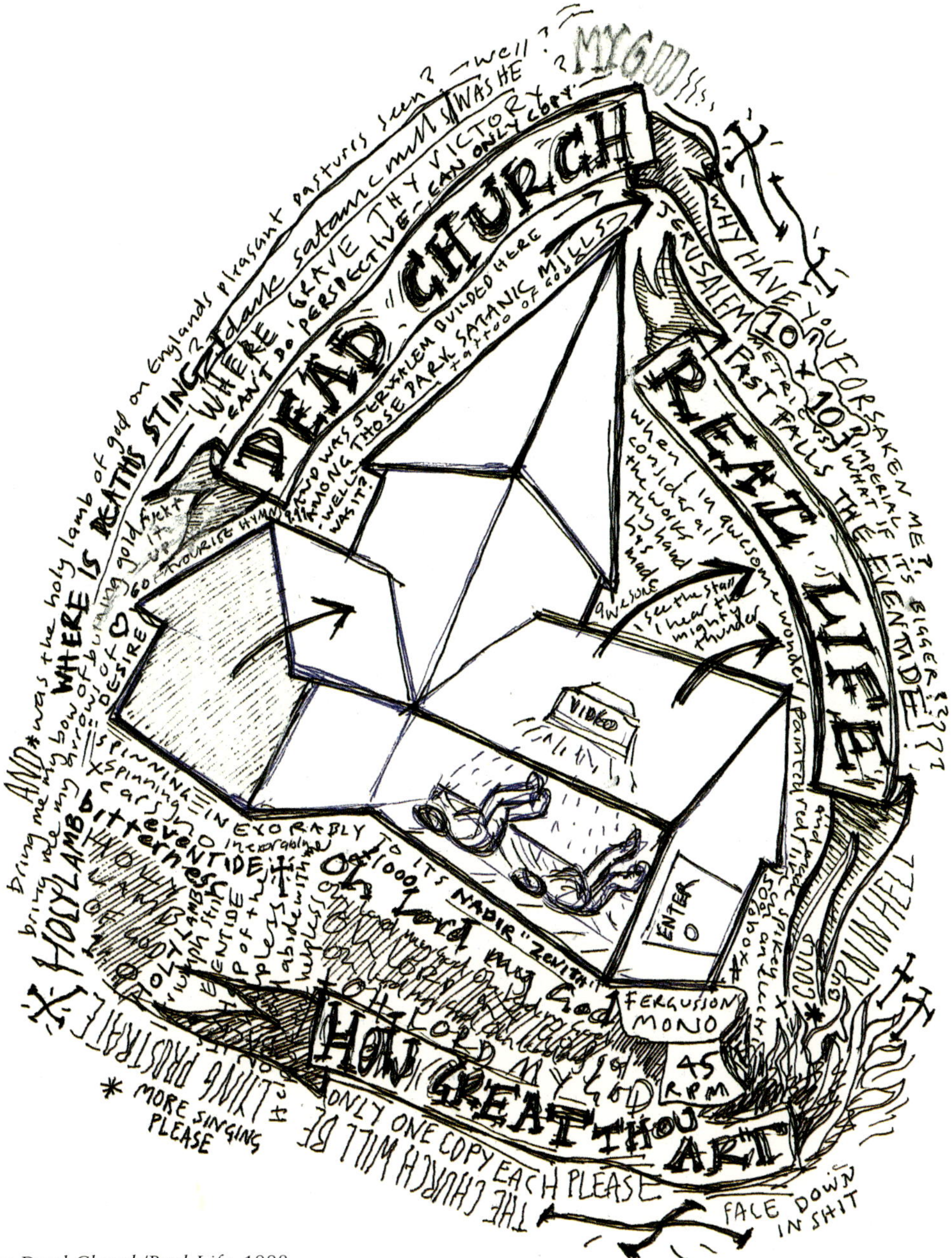


*Sketch for Dead Church/Real Life, 1998*